MW01234868

Tastes and Tales
of a Chef

The Apprentice's Journey

Edward G. Leonard, CMC

PEARSON

Prentice
Hall

Upper Saddle River, New Jersey, 07458

Executive Editor: Vernon R. Anthony
Editorial Assistant: Beth Dyke
Senior Marketing Manager: Ryan DeGrote
Senior Marketing Coordinator: Elizabeth Farrell
Marketing Assistant: Les Roberts
Director of Manufacturing and Production: Bruce Johnson
Managing Editor: Mary Carnis
Production Editor: Ann Mohan, WordCrafters Editorial Services, Inc.
Manufacturing Manager: Ilene Sanford

Manufacturing Buyer: Cathleen Petersen
Creative Director: Cheryl Asherman
Senior Design Coordinator: Miguel Ortiz
Illustrations: Mark Ammerman
Cover Designer: Christopher Weigand
Cover Photograph: American Culinary Federation
Composition: Meridee Mucciarone, WordCrafters Editorial Services, Inc.
Printer/Binder: Phoenix Book Tech
Cover Printer: Phoenix Book Tech

Pearson Education LTD.
Pearson Education, Singapore, Pte. Ltd
Pearson Education, Canada, Ltd
Pearson Education–Japan

Pearson EducationAustralia PTY, Limited
Pearson Education North Asia Ltd
Pearson Educaçion de Mexico, S.A. de C.V
Pearson Education Malaysia, Pte. Ltd

10 9 8 7 6 5 4 3 2 1
ISBN 0-13-119683-9

Contents

Foreword

I became acquainted with Edward Leonard more than 20 years ago at a food competition set up by his then-employer, TrustHouse Forte.

The day I met Chef Ed I knew he was made of Italian marble with some German granite mixed in. His ideas and concepts have become a driving force in our food industry.

While he was an established chef and manager supervising many food and beverage operations and staff, he humbled himself and started again as an apprentice. He put in many hours, days, and years learning his trade and to become a good cook, but his book will tell the tales of the passion that helped him go the extra mile needed to achieve perfection and success.

His common-sense approach has made him what he is today, and his listening skills have helped him absorb new ideas and concepts, which he shares in his book and his lessons.

I am proud to have coached him as he gained success in food competitions and saw him remain humble when he apprenticed with the New York Regional Culinary team in the 1984 Culinary Olympics in Frankfurt, Germany. He went on to become captain of the New York team in 1992, leading it to win the most medals it has ever won as well as two perfect gold scores. His team won the Culinary Classic Cup in May 2003, sweeping all categories.

Today he is repaying his culinary debt by giving back to others and leading our ACF Culinary Team USA 2004 to success.

Always remember: Cooking is an art and a science, and it is a way of sharing.

Frederic "Fritz" Sonnenschmidt, CMC, AAC
(Author of *The Professional Art of Garde Manger*
and *Tastes and Tales of a Chef: Stories and Recipes*)

Foreword

Great food is not just the result of great recipes and ingredients or the surroundings in which it is served. It is the passion of the chefs in the kitchen pouring their love of food and cooking into every dish they prepare. It is said that cooking is an art, and no one knows that better than Certified Master Chef Edward Leonard, who is full of ideas, vision, and passion about the pleasures of the table and the sharing of hospitality.

Chef Leonard has the ability to transform normal, everyday foods into great works of art. He has the greatest respect both for people and for food and dining. He has been inspired by years of experiences and travels in which he's learned from other great chefs.

Taste and Tales of a Chef: The Apprentice's Journey tells part of Chef Leonard's story and what makes up the spirit of this professional chef. Chef Leonard, President of the American Culinary Federation, executive chef of the Westchester Country Club, and world-class culinary champion, craftily weaves his tales and recipes into a story of culinary extravaganza.

When the fire's out, the pots are scrubbed, and the dinner guests have happily departed, who is left behind to savor the taste of success but the chef? As Chef Leonard says:

Yes, into the fire and into the pan
It is my life, my passion, it is who I am.

Enjoy the stories, the recipes, and the personality of one of America's grand chefs. With nothing to else to prove, all that is left to do is pass on to others what he has learned to love so much: good food, good people, good fun, hospitality, sharing, and family.

Mike Baskette
Director of Operations and Education
The American Culinary Federation

Preface

One Must Live to Cook, Not Cook to Live

I dedicate this book to all cooks and culinarians who, due to their passion and love of this craft, have dedicated so much time and effort to their work.

I follow the very tough act of my mentor, Chef Frederic H. Sonnenschmidt.

He wrote the first *Tastes and Tales of a Chef* and has taught me much from my start as an apprentice to my status today of Certified Master Chef.

I hope you enjoy the tales of fun and, in some cases, learn a valuable lesson as well. In addition to enjoying the reading, I hope you will also cook the recipes and feel the passion for that wonderful thing called food.

As a society we have lost the ability to relax and dine to make eating home-cooked meals at the family table a daily requirement instead of a special thing to do. Cooking and the enjoyment of food can and will bring everyone closer together.

My family is from Naples, Italy. I was taught a long time ago that in Italy we live to eat, whereas in other countries people eat to live. Good food is life, and life is good food.

Chef Edward G. Leonard, CMC

Acknowledgments

I want to thank my awesome family for their support, especially my wife Ariadna, who is my steady calm and supports my crazy life and all the endeavors that I do while being my best friend whose recipe for Carnitas Monterey is featured.

To my three children, Edward Christopher, Giancarlo, and Cosette, the lights of my life and my inspiration for still doing all I do.

To my Grandma Civetello, long gone but never forgotten in my heart and in all of my kitchens.

To my many colleagues and friends, who inspire me every day to do all that I love to do.

To my apprentices and chefs, especially Mike, Matt, and Moose, for all the years in Chicago, Connecticut, and New York with Chefs Victor, José, Big Mike, and Jennifer, along with others who have worked so hard for me and will some day leave me for a kitchen of their own. May they carry the passion and flame for cuisine that I have always and keep the culinary pride alive and well.

To Mr. Robert James, CCM, and Mr. Bill Minard for their support of my culinary program at the Westchester Country Club.

To my chefs on the ACF Culinary Team 2004, for they keep reminding me we always learn when we cook together.

Special thanks to Chef Fritz Sonnenschmidt, CMC, for his lessons in cuisine and the lesson to never forget where you come from.

To my chef friends Brad Barnes, CMC, my partner for the CMC exam, my German chef friend Chef Joachim Buchner, CMC, and Chef Steve Jilleba, CMC, who are not only very good cooks but great people as well.

And most of all, thanks to the readers of this book, all the members of the American Culinary Federation, the current board of directors for the ACF—especially Chef Louie Perrotte, who still cooks today at his restaurant Le Coq Au Vin in Orlando—and to Prentice Hall for finding a way to publish a book of cookery with some fun in it.

Chef Edward G. Leonard, CMC
(Cannot Make Consommé)

Tastes and Tales of a Chef

The Apprentice's Journey

Some Myths and Truths About Chefs

Myth: Chefs are always late.
The Truth: Chefs are never late, only delayed.

Myth: Chefs think they are always right.
The Truth: Chefs are not always right; they are just never wrong.

Myth: Chefs never make mistakes.
The Truth: Chefs never make mistakes; they only create something new.

Myth: Chefs are very temperamental.
The Truth: Chefs are very even tempered, but at times very passionate about their food.

Myth: Chefs yell and scream.
The Truth: Chefs do not yell or scream; they only encourage loudly.

Myth: Chefs have huge egos.
Truth: Chefs have confidence in their ability.

Myth: Chefs steal.
Truth: Chefs do not steal; they borrow.

Myth: Chefs are great people; they are kind and have big hearts.
Truth: Chefs are great people; they are kind and have big hearts.

This Thing Called Food

*T*he monk Buddha once made a statement about life that holds very true for the art of cooking: "Your work is to discover your work, and then with all your heart to give yourself to it."

At some point all of us discover that culinary arts is our work or our hobby. To be successful and to become very good cooks, we must give all of our hearts. Cooking, whether at home or for work, is a skill we should love and enjoy. It is a skill that results in good-tasting food that binds us together. It gives us the chance to bring pleasure to those who sit down and enjoy our efforts.

There are some who achieve good results because they have a natural ability to just cook good food. They are like artists with a canvas; they pick up the brush and it flows from them.

I believe that those who really enjoy to cook and bake have no fear and no ego hang-ups. They step into the kitchen to cook, have fun, and please the people they care about with no presumptions. Their unbridled passion for cooking and the excitement of what they are doing with food brings them joy and a sense of pride.

I urge you to practice cooking. Get comfortable with what you are doing, and, more important, have fun in the kitchen. Do not be afraid to create, to try, and to sing with the food you are preparing. The stage for working with food is endless and offers great pleasure to those who cook and bake as well as for those who taste the results. Always remember: An earth-shaking talent is not needed for a person to love to cook, read a cookbook, or just go out to eat and let others do the cooking.

Unfortunately, cooking has become a flavor of the moment. It revolves around spending the most money to open the biggest and hottest new place to dine. It has become a way of life even for youngsters who are caught up in watching cooking shows and yearning for cooking lessons or chef-teaching birthday parties. Specialty markets are on the rise, charging huge sums of money for high-quality food that in Europe is just part of everyday life for the chef and the housewife alike. Cookbooks are issued monthly, and new books are always in production. Chefs and cooks are celebrities.

All for this simple thing called food that has shaped life, countries, cultures, and people all over the world. Perhaps one day the insanity will stop and an honest respect for food and for those who produce it from the home and commercial venues will come to be.

The Journey from Apprentice to Master Chef

The journey from apprentice to chef is many things. No matter how much you have packed, you will need something else. No matter how well you believe you are doing on your journey, you will soon find out otherwise.

What you learn during that journey can shape your future, and how you respond to what you learn will build your character. My journey began as an eager apprentice willing to learn and do what it takes to be a Certified Master Chef (CMC). Even though I have earned this thing called CMC and my apprenticeship has been long over, the journey continues. I am still learning lessons, and the journey still takes me to great places and fills my life with passion, excitement, disappointment, and the yearning for more.

I will never forget the thrill I had sitting with my Grandma Civetello listening to the stories of the old country (Italy) while eating a half a loaf of fresh-baked Italian bread, dipping it in her gravy. (Gravy is what Americans call tomato sauce.) Her gravy was so good at times that no pasta was wanted or needed.

I remember the meatballs, so light and flavorful, cooking in the oil. I remember homemade pasta and Sunday suppers with more food than the whole block could eat. Food was part of life; it was something that brought everyone together. Whether we were fighting, debating, or celebrating, food was the center of attention.

I learned then that great dishes came from someone's mom, grandmother, grandfather, or family member. From that time on I wanted to cook, to be a craftsman, working with the products of the earth, land, and sea. It was my calling, I said to myself. And there the journey of a young apprentice filled with the hope of chefdom began.

One day when I was helping Grandma with the gravy and the meatballs, I made the mistake of adding touches of my own that I thought would help the cause. Well, my touches of more of this and that did not help. That's when the wooden spoon came out. I learned that it did more than just stir the sauce, and I learned some Italian not quite for public use. It was then that I also discovered that an apprentice had to learn before he could create!

Reader's Notes and Thoughts

Mignonette Sauce

Ingredients

1/2 cup	Very clean minced shallots
2 oz.	Very finely chopped chives
2/3 cup	Champagne vinegar
1/2 tsp.	Fresh cracked black pepper

Method

Mix items very well.
Let sit at least one hour.

Sauce Rémoulade

Ingredients

6 oz.	Sweet pickles, finely chopped
2 tbsp.	Capers
4	White anchovies, finely minced
2 oz.	Parsley, chopped
2/3 oz.	Chervil, chopped
2/3 oz.	Tarragon, chopped
2 tbsp.	Stone ground mustard
1 1/2 qts.	Mayonnaise
To taste	Salt and pepper
1–2 pinches	Cayenne pepper
1–2 oz.	Pickle juice
2 tbsp.	Lime juice

Method

Combine all ingredients.
Mix well.
Adjust seasoning.

Chef Leonard's Special Sauce
for Reuben and Other Sandwiches

Ingredients

1 pt.	Hellmann's mayonnaise
4 medium	Hardboiled eggs, diced
6 oz.	Tanqueray cocktail sauce
1/2 cup	Sweet relish
2 oz.	Minced onion, sautéed
3 oz.	Sour cream
2 tbsp.	Extra virgin olive oil
2 tbsp.	Parsley, chopped

Method

Combine all ingredients.
Mix well.

Eggnog Dressing

Ingredients

2 cups	Eggnog
1/2 cup	Mayonnaise
1/2 cup	Olive oil
1 1/2 tsp.	Sea salt or kosher salt
8 oz.	Champagne or pear wine vinegar
To taste	White pepper

Method

Whisk all items together well.
Adjust seasoning.

Orange Vinaigrette

Ingredients

2 cups	Fresh orange juice
1 cup	Extra virgin olive oil
1 cup	Grapeseed oil
1 cup	Champagne vinegar
2 tsp.	Mint, finely chopped
To taste	Sugar
To taste	Salt and pepper

Method

Blend juices with oil using a blender stick.
Whip in remaining items.
Adjust seasoning as needed.

Citrus Vinaigrette

Ingredients

1 cup	Fresh lime juice
$1/2$ cup	Fresh lemon juice
2 cups	Fresh orange juice
$1/2$ cup	Fresh grapefruit juice
1 cup	Grapeseed oil
2 cups	Champagne or pear vinegar
1 cup	Simple syrup
4 tbsp.	Fresh sage, minced
To taste	Salt and pepper

Method

Blend juices with oil using a blender stick.
Whip in remaining items.
Adjust seasoning as needed.

The Best Chicken Salad
(8 servings)

Ingredients

1½ lb.	Roasted chicken meat, diced small
4 stalks	Celery, peeled and diced
1	Shredded apple
	Juice of 1 lemon
2 tsp.	Poultry seasoning
2½ cups	Mayonnaise
2 oz.	Extra virgin olive oil
To taste	Kosher salt
To taste	Freshly ground black pepper
2 tbsp.	Parsley, chopped
2 tsp.	Tarragon, minced

Method

Combine all ingredients.
Mix well.
Adjust seasoning.

Mark Ammerman 2004

Pots and Pans

My first apprentice job was at a private club in New Haven, Connecticut. It was nothing more than a potwasher's job, but it was a chance to be in an exclusive kitchen that catered many high-profile events.

My first week was not so good. The water used to wash and rinse the pots was very hot, and my hands, needless to say, were not used to this. On my second day, the chef yelled that he needed more sauté pans. I, being the eager new employee wanting to impress the chef, ran to the pot area and quickly came back with six pans. They were saucepans, not sauté pans. The chef proceeded to grab every sauté pan in the house and dump it into the sink. I was to wash and dry each one until I learned what a sauté pan was.

After this rough start, however, the chef took a liking to me, and we spoke often of food, his career, and everything culinary. I told the chef that the buffets he did on Sunday were just incredible and that it would be an honor to work the buffet with him as his assistant. He said, "This would be good. I could use a runner to get me things and you get to learn at the same time."

I was so excited and proud that first Sunday when I put on a chef coat, apron, and hat and worked with the chef. Man, how great was I—helping the chef after only two weeks of work! After the buffet was over I felt so good about myself. I even got to carve the meat for the club members. I said to myself, "Only two weeks and look at this; I will be off the pot sink soon enough!"

We had something to eat, and then we all went back into the kitchen. The chefs had cleaned up and were ready to leave. I looked over at the pot-washing area and saw a huge number of pots, pans, and utensils all piled up. The floor and sink were a mess. I thought, "Wow, the poor person doing those pots is in for a long night."

I was shortly to learn that the poor person was me. As the chef started to leave, he said, "Leonard, what are you waiting for? Get on those pots now and get this place cleaned up!"

I stammered a bit, but to no avail.

The chef said, "I hired you for one job. You want me to teach you so you can learn? I will do that. However, that is on your own time until I feel you are ready to be part of the kitchen brigade."

Lesson learned: Never count your chickens before they are hatched.

Lobster Newburg
(6 servings)

Ingredients

6 tbsp.	Butter
3 cups	Cooked lobster, cut in 2-inch pieces
1/3 cup	Madeira or dry sherry
1 1/2 cups	Heavy cream
5	Egg yolks
3/4 tsp.	Salt
1/8 tsp.	Cayenne pepper
1/2 tsp.	Lemon juice
6	Patty shells, or 2–3 cups steamed rice or 8–12 buttered toast points
Optional	Paprika

Method

In large skillet, melt butter. Add lobster meat and stir constantly for 1 minute.

Add Madeira or sherry and 1 cup heavy cream. Bring to a boil while stirring.

Reduce heat to lowest point, still stirring, and cook for 2 minutes.

Beat the egg yolks into the remaining ½ cup cream.

Beat into this mixture 4 tbsp. of simmering lobster sauce.

Then, in a slow stream, pour the mixture back into the skillet, stirring constantly.

Cook over moderate heat until the sauce thickens. Do not allow to boil.

Season with salt, cayenne, and lemon juice.

Serve in patty shells or over steamed rice or warm toast points.

Roast Stuffed Pork Chops
with Applejack Cream Sauce
(4 servings)

Stuffing

Ingredients

4 tbsp.	Butter
1/4 cup	Onion, finely chopped
2	Pork sausages coarsely chopped
1 1/2 cups	Day-old bread, diced in 1/2-inch cubes
1/2 cup	Peeled, cored and diced apple, cut into 1/2-inch cubes
1 tbsp.	Parsley
To taste	Salt
To taste	Freshly ground black pepper

Method

Melt 2 tbsp. butter; add chopped onion and sausage meat.
Cook 3–4 minutes, reserve.
To same pan, add 2 tbsp. butter and the diced bread.
Cook 3–4 minutes.
Add diced bread to reserved sausage, and mix in apples and parsley.
Add salt and pepper to taste.

Pork Chops

Ingredients

4	Center-cut pork chops, 1–1 1/2 inch thick
2 tbsp.	Butter, softened
4 strips	Bacon, cut in half
1/2 cup	Applejack
1/2 cup	Chicken stock
1/4 cup	Heavy cream

Method

Wash pork chops, pat dry.

Season with salt and pepper and rub with butter.

Slice a pocket in each pork chop then fill with stuffing. Do not pack and secure with twine or toothpick.

Drape bacon strips over chops and roast in 375° oven for 30 minutes.

Season with salt and pepper.

Sauce

Heat ¼ cup applejack until lukewarm and set it alight with a match.

Pour over chops.

When flames have ceased baste the chops and return to oven for 10–12 minutes or until chops are brown and fully cooked.

Remove chops from the rack.

Pour the chicken stock and remaining applejack into the roasting pan and bring to a boil on top of stove for 2–3 minutes, scraping brown bits.

Stir in cream, bring to boil once more, and season with salt and pepper.

Apple and Wild Rice Griddle Cakes
(8–12 servings)

Ingredients

2 cups	All-purpose flour
2 tsp.	Baking powder
2 tsp.	Sugar
1 tsp.	Salt
3	Eggs, lightly beaten
1 cup	Milk
1 cup	Buttermilk
1/3 cup	Melted butter
1 cup	Wild rice, fully cooked
1/2 cup	Apples, diced small and cooked in some butter and a touch of maple syrup, then cooled

Method

Sift dry items and place in bowl.
Make a well in center.
Pour in eggs, milk, and buttermilk.
With a wooden spoon, mix enough to just blend.
Add rice, butter, and apples; stir in carefully; do not overmix.
Cook in a cast iron skillet or nonstick pan with 1/2 oz. of butter.

Southern Fried Chicken with Cream Gravy
(4 servings)

Chicken

Ingredients

2¹/₂ lbs.	Frying chicken, cut into serving pieces
2 cups	Buttermilk
2 tbsp.	Salt
1 cup	Flour
3 tbsp.	Spice de Cosette seasoning
1 cup	Lard
or	
¹/₂ cup	Vegetable shortening combined with ½ cup lard

Method

Sprinkle chicken with salt and cover with buttermilk. Let sit overnight.
Drain well and pat dry.
In a sturdy paper bag, place flour and seasoning. Add chicken and shake
bag to distribute evenly.
Remove chicken, shake it free of excess flour, and place on wax paper.
Over high heat, melt lard or combined lard and shortening to depth of
¹/₄ inch in a heavy skillet; add more as needed.
Add chicken, skin side down. Cover skillet and fry for 6–8 minutes until
golden brown.
Turn chicken over and cover pot again, frying until golden brown.
Place on a pan and put into a warm oven until gravy is made.

Cream Gravy

Ingredients

2 tbsp.	Flour
³/₄ cup	Chicken stock
¹/₂ – ³/₄ cup	Light cream
To taste	Salt
To taste	White pepper

Method

Pour off all but 2 tbsp. of fat from the skillet and add 2 tbsp. of flour; stir until combined.

Add chicken stock and ½ cup light cream and cook over moderate heat, beating with a whisk until the gravy is smooth and thick.

If a thinner gravy is desired, add more cream.

Season to taste with salt and pepper and serve with fried chicken.

Italian Cheese Pie
(8 servings)

Crust

Ingredients

1¹/₂ cups	Flour
1¹/₄ tsp.	Baking powder
¹/₂ tsp.	Salt
3 tbsp.	Butter
¹/₄ cup	Sugar
1	Egg
¹/₂ tsp.	Vanilla
¹/₂ tsp.	Grated orange peel
1 tbsp.	Orange juice

Method

Beat butter, sugar, and egg until light and fluffy.
Beat in orange peel, vanilla, and juice.
Mix all dry ingredients together and sift.
Add half of flour mixture to egg mixture, beat until well blended, knead in remaining half.
Let dough sit for 1 hour in refrigerator.
Roll out into a 9-inch pie tin.
Save remaining dough to cut strips for a lattice top after you pour in the filling.

Filling

Ingredients

16 oz.	Hand-dipped ricotta
³/₄ cup	Sugar
3	Eggs
1 tsp.	Vanilla
¹/₂ cup	Mustard fruits, diced (optional)

Method

In bowl, beat ricotta until creamy.
Fold in all other ingredients until well combined.
Pour into crust and use the reserved dough to make strips for a lattice top.
Bake at 350° about 40–50 minutes until set.
Let cool overnight.

White Chocolate and Strawberry Decadence
(8 servings)

Turnover

Ingredients

2 sheets	Puff pastry
1	Egg wash
8 servings	Your favorite recipe white chocolate mousse or a quality packaged mix

Method

Using crinkle cutter, cut puff pastry sheets into 8 triangles with 4-inch sides.
Brush with egg wash, prick with a fork, and place on baking sheet.
Bake at 350° until raised and done. Leave to cool.

Note: For egg wash, beat 2 eggs and combine with 1 tbsp. milk to give dough a nice brown and shiny finish.

Strawberry Filling

Ingredients

2 pts.	Strawberries, hulled
1 tsp.	Pure vanilla extract
3 oz.	Brown sugar

Method

Slice strawberries and mix with brown sugar and vanilla.
Allow to sit for 10 minutes.

Strawberry Sauce

Ingredients

1 pt.	Strawberries, hulled
2 tbsp.	Sugar

Method

Roughly cut strawberries and sprinkle with sugar.
Puree and pass through a fine sieve.
Chill until ready to serve.

Garnish

Ingredients

4 oz.	Semi-sweet chocolate, melted
8	Chocolate leaves
8 oz.	Heavy cream

To Assemble the Decadence

Prepare mousse in accordance with package directions or recipe.
Slice puff pastry triangles in half to create two layers.
Stuff with strawberry filling. Pipe a small rosette of mousse; sandwich back together.
Drizzle with melted chocolate.
Pipe rosette of white chocolate mousse on top; add chocolate leaf.
Serve on strawberry sauce; dot with quantity of heavy cream and pull with toothpick to give teardrop effect.

Reader's Notes and Thoughts

The Soup Paddle

My first true study of the culinary arts took place at a vocational school in a program that was the first of its kind. We cooked the meals for all the students and teachers in a private dining room setting. Both the production and the fine dining aspects were challenging and taught us a lot.

Our two chefs were former instructors from the Culinary Institute of America (CIA) when it was in New Haven, Connecticut. The head instructor and department head was a talented chef and a former army master chef from Italy. He was tough and old school. He did take an interest in some students, which could be good or bad. I was one of them. He had a strong accent and a particular manner of speaking, especially when upset.

There were some girls in our class that I took a fancy to. One day I was working on some cold food platters and decorations, making apple birds, carving melons, and so forth. Two of the girls came by and said, "Wow, how do you make those? They are so beautiful!" This was so cool; the girls were flirting and wanting me to teach them this chef school stuff!

After a while we all just started talking and flirting and having a nice time. I was leaning over the counter and doing my best to impress the young ladies. All of a sudden I felt this big sting against my backside and heard a loud "whack" sound. I must have jumped 10 feet in the air. The girls went away laughing.

There stood my chef with a large wooden soup paddle in his hands and giving me a not-so-pleased look. He stared into my eyes sternly and said, "Leonard, you make up your mind in my class. It is cooking or chasing girls? You decide. Will you be a shoemaker or a Casanova?"

After much embarrassment, not to mention pain, I decided that learning to cook would be better for my career *and* my behind.

Chicken Provençale
(6 servings)

Ingredients

5 each	Chicken suprêmes (boneless, skinless breasts with the first wing segment attached)
1/4 tsp.	Salt, to taste
1/8 teaspoon	Pepper, to taste
1 1/2 oz.	Flour
1 1/2 fluid oz.	Vegetable oil
2 1/2 oz.	Butter
1 1/2 each	Garlic cloves, minced
5 fluid oz.	White wine
1 lb.	Tomato concassée (peeled, seeded, and diced)
2 oz.	Black olives, sliced or julienned
1 1/2 each	Anchovy fillets, mashed to a paste
1 tbsp.	Basil, chiffonade (finely shredded)

Method

Season the chicken suprêmes with salt and pepper. Dredge them lightly with flour, shaking off excess.

Heat the vegetable oil in a sauté pan and sauté the chicken breasts until golden brown and cooked through.

Remove the breasts from the pan and keep warm.

Pour off excess fat from the sauté pan; add the butter. Return the pan to the heat. Add the garlic to the melted butter and sauté it briefly. Deglaze the pan with the wine, stirring well to release all of the drippings.

Add the tomato concassée, olives, and anchovy paste. Bring this mixture to a simmer and cook it for a few minutes or until the flavor is developed.

Return the chicken breasts along with any released juices to the sauté pan and toss to coat the chicken with the sauce.

Serve the chicken with the sauce on a heated plate. Garnish with the basil.

Chef Ed's Low-Fat Spiced Turkey Patties
(4 servings)

Ingredients

1 lb.	Cooked rice
2 oz.	Cream
1 lb.	Ground turkey meat
2 oz.	Shallots, minced
1 oz.	Sage, chopped
1/2 oz.	Garlic, minced
1/2 oz.	Dijon mustard
1/2 tsp.	Chili paste
1/2 oz.	Worcestershire sauce
To taste	Salt

Method

Cover rice with cream and let sit 15 minutes.
Mix all other ingredients well.
Add rice and form into 8-oz. patties.
Cook in a nonstick pan until brown on both sides.
Finish in 350° oven for 2–3 minutes.
Top with favorite sandwich sauce, dressing, etc.

Note: Great on flavor, low in fat.

Pork Scaloppini Marsala
(5 servings)

Ingredients

1¹/₂ lb.	Pork tenderloins, cut into 2-oz. portions
As needed	Flour, seasoned
1¹/₂ oz.	Butter
2 each	Shallots, minced
5 fluid oz.	Marsala, dry
5 fluid oz.	Brown sauce
2 oz.	Butter
¹/₄ tsp.	Salt, to taste
¹/₈ tsp.	Pepper, to taste

Method

Cut pork into scaloppini. Flatten pork with a mallet to an even thickness.
Dredge pork in flour and sauté on both sides in butter until lightly
browned.
When pork is done, remove from pan and keep warm.
Add shallots to pan and sauté until translucent.
Add wine and reduce by one-half.
Add brown sauce and reduce until sauce consistency is reached.
Remove from heat and finish with butter. Season.
Serve sauce over the pork

Beef Stroganoff
(6 servings)

Ingredients

2 lbs.	Tenderloin of beef, cut into small dice
1 1/2 fluid oz.	Vegetable oil, as needed
1/4 lb.	Mushrooms, sliced
1 oz.	Butter
4 oz.	Onions, minced
1/2 pt.	Brown sauce
4 fluid oz.	Sour cream
1/2 tbsp.	Dijon mustard
1/2 tbsp.	Lemon juice
1/4 tsp.	Salt, to taste
1/4 tsp.	Pepper, to taste

Method

Sauté beef in hot oil to desired doneness. Remove meat and keep warm.
Sauté mushrooms in butter for 2–3 minutes and remove.
Sauté onions in butter until translucent.
Add brown sauce and simmer 10 minutes.
Add sour cream to pan, stirring constantly. Reduce until proper consistency is reached.
Add mustard and lemon juice and adjust seasoning to taste with salt and pepper.
Reheat meat and mushrooms in sauce (do not boil meat in sauce).

Sweet Noodle Pie
(8 servings)

Ingredients

16-oz. package	Egg noodles, cooked
2 lbs.	Fresh ricotta
3/4 cup	Sugar
2 oz.	Butter
6	Eggs
1/2 qt.	Milk
1/2 qt.	Heavy cream
2 tsp.	Real vanilla
1 cup	Maraschino cherries

Method

Melt butter.
Mix all ingredients in a bowl well.
Place in a well-buttered 9 × 9 inch baking pan and bake at 350° until set in the middle.

Frittata
(6 servings)

Ingredients

12	Eggs, large
1 oz.	Olive oil
As needed	Parsley, chopped
As needed	Kosher salt
As needed	Black pepper, ground
4 oz.	Light cream
1 oz.	Olive oil blend
6 oz.	Onions, diced medium
8 oz.	Zucchini, diced
8 oz.	Roasted red pepper, julienned
12 oz.	Potatoes, cooked and diced
As needed	Fresh basil, finely julienned
As needed	Sage, chopped
8 oz.	Mozzarella, shredded

Method

Mix first six ingredients well and reserve.
Sauté olive oil blend, onions, zucchini, and red pepper in hot oil until firm but tender.
Remove from heat.
Mix potatoes with herbs, cheese, and vegetables.
Place equal amounts of potato and vegetable mixture into 6 greased casserole dishes or a large oven skillet.
Ladle eggs over mixture and bake in 350° oven until center is cooked.

The Curse of the Hollandaise

One of the most debated sauces is hollandaise, a rich sauce of egg yolks, clarified butter, a touch of lemon juice, salt, and Tabasco. Some say it is terrible to put an egg sauce over eggs, as with the famous dish Eggs Benedict. But love it or hate it, hollandaise is a part of classical cuisine and a mother sauce (a group of five sauces that are the foundation of sauce making). It has many versions and can be made with herbs, reductions, tomatoes, and other ingredients.

Making hollandaise is a challenge, especially if you are making a large amount. First you have to beat the yolks over a double boiler, and if this is not done right, you will make scrambled eggs. Then, if you add too much butter or if you add the butter too fast or it's too hot, you can break the sauce (meaning it will curdle or turn to scrambed eggs).

One day in school, we had a large breakfast function. My job was to make the hollandaise sauce for 150 people. I remember Chef showing me the procedure step by step. I watched with amazement as the eggs turned to a wonderful yellow, silky concoction with the consistency of a ribbon. He added the butter and a dash of salt and hot sauce, and wow, what a tasty, creamy, sauce! The issue here was that he used only four eggs. Four eggs to yield a sauce for eight? I had to make it for 150 people.

I had questions. I needed answers. I received nothing. I was told, "You were taught, now get to work."

My first attempt was not so good. The heat got too hot, and I did not whip the yolks the right way or fast enough. Instead of a great hollandaise for 150, I had scrambled eggs for 150. Then I managed to spill 6 of the 12 pounds of melted butter all over me, and I had to make a quick change in the locker room without Chef seeing me.

After I changed, I could hear the chef nearby barking, "How is that sauce coming?" You've never seen a person make egg sandwiches and wrap them so fast in your life!

My second attempt, made with very tired arms, turned out bad as well. There was too much butter and my sauce started to break—as did I, becoming terror struck as the chef reentered the kitchen.

He glanced over and saw what was becoming a mess. He started to push me aside. As he did, I hit the bowl and broken hollandaise sauce flew up on you-know-who.

"Leonard!" he yelled, along with some things that cannot be put in this book. "I taught you; now do it the right way and clean up this mess."

After cleaning up and feeling that perhaps a career of another sort would suit me better, I started to crack and separate another 80 eggs. This time, tired arms and all, the groove was there and I finished a huge batch of the tastiest and smoothest hollandaise there ever was. Chef came by, took the tasting spoon, inspected the sauce, muttered something, and placed the spoon in his mouth. A smile, though a slight one, came across his face. He turned, and as he walked away he gave me a punch in the arm (a sign that I did well). He just said, "Get to the dining room quickly."

In the dining room the poached eggs, crisp muffins, and nicely browned Canadian bacon awaited. Those eggs, that bacon, and those muffins were about to be covered in pure heaven. My sauce would be the hit of the day.

I placed my bowl of sauce on the counter. Guests started arriving, and the chef went to work. As he turned he bumped into a student, who then fell back and knocked over my bowl of hollandaise. The chef thought I was about to lose it. He looked at me and said, "Leonard, why, why, why?"

I asked myself the same question. Could this be my fault? Was I not meant to be a chef? Was my presence causing havoc in the kitchen, or was it just the curse of the hollandaise?

Because of this incident, my chefs and cooks make the hollandaise in my kitchens. I stay far away, never to whip those yolks or have them jinx my kitchen again. To this day, Eggs Benedict causes me to shiver and worry that the curse will return.

Basic Hollandaise
(8 servings)

Ingredients

2/3 cup	Water
2 tbsp.	Lemon juice
A touch	White vinegar
1 tsp.	Salt
1/3 tsp.	Cayenne pepper
6	Egg yolks
12 oz.	Melted unsalted butter

Method

In a saucepan, combine water, lemon juice, vinegar, salt, and pepper. Reduce to half.

In a stainless bowl over a double boiler set on medium low heat, add water and egg yolks and whisk until yolks become very thick and like a ribbon.

Remove from heat and slowly stream in the melted butter, whisking quickly until all butter is absorbed and the sauce is smooth.

Adjust seasoning, if desired, with salt, cayenne pepper, and a bit more lemon juice.

Keep in warm area (no more than 140°), covered.

Tomato Hollandaise
(8 servings)

Ingredients

¹/₃ cup	Water
¹/₃ cup	Tomato juice
2 tbsp.	Lemon Juice
A touch	White vinegar
1 tsp.	Salt
¹/₃ tsp.	Cayenne pepper
6	Egg yolks
12 oz.	Melted unsalted butter
1 tbsp.	Fresh basil, chopped
3 tbsp.	Tomatoes, peeled, seeded, diced small

Method

In a saucepan, combine water, tomato juice, lemon juice, vinegar, salt, and pepper.

Reduce to half.

In a stainless bowl over a double boiler set on medium low heat, add water and egg yolks and whisk until yolks become very thick and like a ribbon.

Remove from heat and slowly stream in the melted butter, whisking quickly until all butter is absorbed and the sauce is smooth.

Fold in the basil and tomatoes.

Adjust seasoning, if desired, with salt.

Keep in warm area, (no more than 140°), covered.

Note: Use this sauce for grilled or roasted chicken or a hearty grilled fish such as swordfish.

Eggs Princess
(Named after my wife!)
(8 servings)

Ingredients

24 oz.	Lump crabmeat
3 oz.	Butter
To taste	Salt and pepper
1/2 tsp.	Fresh thyme, minced
16	Eggs, soft poached
16	Brioche circles or English muffin halves, toasted
32	Asparagus spears, blanched
1 oz.	Butter
1	Lemon, cut in half and seeded
1	Recipe of Hollandaise sauce

Method

Sauté the crabmeat in a hot pan with the butter until warm.
Add thyme, salt, and pepper and toss together.
Heat asparagus in a pan with butter and the juice from the lemon; reserve.
On 8 plates, line up 2 brioche or muffin halves per plate
Place equal amounts of the crabmeat on each muffin or brioche half.
Place a poached egg on each half and top with hot hollandaise sauce.
Top each half with two asparagus spears.
Serve.

Eggs Edwardian
(8 servings)

Ingredients

16 oz.	Roasted chicken meat, shredded
2 oz.	Butter
1 oz.	Extra virgin olive oil
8 oz.	Roasted peppers, diced
To taste	Salt and pepper
$1/2$ tsp.	Fresh sage, minced
16	Eggs, soft poached
8 slices	Italian bread (about 3-inch diameter), grilled
16	Slices plum tomatoes cut $1/4$ inch thick
1 oz.	Extra virgin olive oil
$1/2$ tsp.	Oregano
1	Recipe of tomato hollandaise sauce

Method

Sauté the chicken meat in a hot pan with the butter, olive oil, and peppers until hot.

Add sage, salt, and pepper and toss together.

Grill tomatoes in a pan after brushing them with olive oil; season with salt and oregano; reserve.

On 8 plates, line up 1 slice of grilled bread per plate.

Place equal amounts of the chicken and peppers on the bread.

Place two poached eggs on each slice of bread and top with hot hollandaise sauce.

Top each egg with a slice of broiled tomato.

Serve.

Sea Scallops Benedict
with White Truffle Essence Hollandaise
(4 servings)

Truffle Hollandaise

Ingredients

3	Egg yolks
4 oz.	Vinegar
1 tsp.	Truffle paste
1/2 tbsp.	Truffle oil, black
4 oz.	Clarified butter
1–2 tbsp.	Lemon juice
1 tsp.	Fresh thyme
To taste	Salt and pepper

Method

Follow instructions for basic hollandaise sauce.

Sea Scallops Benedict

Ingredients

4 large	Sea scallops
	Note: Ask your fish store for U-8 or U-10 scallops.
2 tbsp.	Olive oil
4 medium	Eggs, fried
4	English muffin bottoms, toasted
4 slices	Pancetta, cooked
1 tbsp.	Tomatoes, diced

Method

Sauté scallops in a hot pan 2–3 minutes on each side.
On each plate, place a muffin half, then the pancetta, then the fried egg.
Top each egg with the scallop.
Pour the cooked and warm hollandaise sauce over the egg.
Garnish with tomatoes.

This makes a rich and tasty breakfast or lunch treat.

BBQ Blender Hollandaise

Ingredients

4	Egg yolks, pasteurized, room temperature
	Juice of 1 lemon
1 tbsp.	Water, hot
2 tsp.	Hot sauce
Pinch	Salt
8 oz.	Butter, melted and very warm (about 140°)
2 oz.	Your favorite BBQ sauce, heated until very hot

Method

Place yolks in blender.

Add lemon juice, water, hot sauce, and salt.

Pulse blender until yolks are frothy.

While blender is running slowly, add hot butter until sauce starts to thicken.

Slowly add BBQ sauce.

Remove from blender and serve.

Reader's Notes and Thoughts

Cry of the Onions

*I*was well on the way to being an apprenticeship and off pot duty for good. I believe the chef had a liking for me, even though he was tough at times. I worked hard learning and doing whatever was needed in the three kitchens we had.

The worst thing about starting as an apprentice is the mundane work you always have to do: peel carrots, peel onions, dice carrots, tourney, carrots and so on. But practicing peeling, dicing, slicing, and special cuts builds your skill level and helps you master these things. Yes, a master at peeling onions. What a great attribute to the kitchen and my résumé!

Being put in a corner or at a table with other apprentices and 50-pound bags of vegetables made for a long and not-so-exciting day. I always said that if you have to spend so much time doing this type of work, you also need to have fun. To this day, as much as I take the standards of my kitchen and the quality of my cuisine seriously, I try to create a fun atmosphere with some moments of laughter here and there.

One day before a big weekend, we were given 150 pounds of onions to peel, dice, and slice for the chefs and cooks. The worst thing about onions is the way they can bring you to tears. Unfortunately, this most-needed vegetable contains sulfur compounds and oils that are pleasing to the taste but hard on the eyes.

Well, as we were going along, many tears were shed by three of the six apprentices peeling. It was time, I thought, to add some humor, so I got three hamburger buns and said, "Hey guys, if you each place a half a bun in your mouth one third of the way, the bun acts as a filter for the onions and you will not cry."

After I did some convincing and explained that the chef had taught me this, each of the apprentices took a half a bun, placed it in his mouth, and went back to onion duty. I loved it! They looked as silly as can be, and each had a puzzled look on his face.

As I walked over to the walk-in, the chef came by with the general manager. You should have seen their faces looking at five apprentices working with buns sticking out of their mouths.

The chef asked, "What in the world is going on here? What is wrong with you guys?" They explained the problem and the great solution that Chef had taught the lead apprentice. I heard a yell of "Leonard, in my office, now!"

Hot water? Yes. Was it fun? You bet! Cooking needs to be fun at times; it makes for better food. A happy cook is a good cook.

Red Onion Relish

Ingredients

12	Red onions, slivered
4 oz.	Butter
1 oz.	Olive oil
2 oz.	Brown sugar
$1/2$ cup	Red wine vinegar
$1/2$ cup	Red wine

Method

Start sautéing onions in large sauté pan with butter and oil.
Add sugar and sauté until onions start to caramelize.
Add vinegar and cook until almost evaporated.
Add wine and reduce until evaporated.
Let cool; do not refrigerate.

Three-Onion Soup
(6 servings)

Ingredients

10 oz.	White onion, thinly sliced
5 oz.	Red onion, thinly sliced
5 oz.	Shallots, thinly sliced
2 oz.	Butter
2 oz.	Lard or olive oil
1 oz.	Flour
2 oz.	Sherry
1 qt.	Beef broth
2 cups	Chicken broth
To taste	Salt and pepper

Method

Brown onions in a 2-quart soup pot with the butter and oil until very soft and nicely caramelized.

Add flour and mix in well, cooking over low heat 1–2 minutes.

Add sherry and stir.

Add both broths, mix well, and bring to a boil.

Reduce heat and let simmer 30–45 minutes.

Adjust seasoning and serve with croutons.

Creamy Five-Onion Soup
(8 servings)

Ingredients

5 oz.	Small red onions, diced
8 oz.	Small white onions, diced
8 oz.	Small yellow onions, diced
4 oz.	Shallots, diced
5 oz.	Leeks, diced
2 oz.	Butter
2 oz.	Olive oil
5 oz.	Flour
2 oz.	Sherry
1 qt. plus 1 cup	Chicken broth
2 cups	Heavy cream
1 oz.	Butter
1/2 cup	Grated parmesan cheese

Method

In a 4-quart soup pan, heat oil and butter.
Add all onions and cook until very soft and lightly browned.
Add flour and cook for 2–3 minutes.
Add sherry and mix well.
Add chicken broth and stir well; bring to a boil.
Reduce heat and let simmer for 45 minutes.
Heat cream in a saucepan with 1 oz. butter.
With a blending stick or large blender, mix soup with cream and blend until smooth.
Place on very low heat and simmer for 10 minutes.
Whisk in cheese, season with salt and pepper, and serve.

Polenta with Sausage
(6 servings)

Polenta

Ingredients

1½ cups	Milk
½ tsp.	Dried basil
¼ tsp.	Dried thyme
3 tbsp.	Butter
¾ cup	Yellow cornmeal
To taste	Salt and pepper

Method

Bring milk, herbs, and butter to a boil in a heavy-bottomed saucepan.
While stirring, slowly add cornmeal.
Whisk on a low heat for 10–12 minutes until polenta is smooth and starts to thicken.
Season.
Pour into a 10-inch pie pan or casserole lightly coated with olive oil.
Reserve.

Topping

Ingredients

2 tbsp.	Olive oil
1 cup	Onion, diced
3 cloves	Garlic, sliced
½ cup	Carrots, diced small
10 oz.	Ground sausage meat
2 tbsp.	Virgin olive oil
1½ cups	Cremini mushrooms, sliced
½ cup	Red wine
8 oz.	Chicken broth
3–4 tbsp.	Roasted veal demi-glace
1½ cups	Roma tomatoes, diced
2 tbsp.	Fresh basil, chopped

1 tbsp.	Fresh sage, chopped
3 tbsp.	Parsley, chopped
2 pinches	Crushed red pepper
To taste	Kosher salt
1/2 cup	Grated Parmesan cheese
1/4 cup	Seasoned bread crumbs

Method

Heat olive oil in heavy skillet.

Add onions, garlic, and carrots, and cook until tender and lightly brown.

Add sausage and cook until meat is almost cooked.

Add oil and mushrooms and cook 2–3 minutes.

Add red wine and simmer for 2–3 minutes.

Add broth and demi-glace.

Stir and simmer 3–4 minutes and add tomatoes, herbs, and seasonings.

Score top of polenta, spread topping evenly, and sprinkle with cheese and breadcrumbs.

Bake in a 350° oven for 15–20 minutes.

Pecan Shrimp, Crab, and Asparagus Salad
(4 servings)

Pecan Dressing

Ingredients

1 oz.	Lemon juice
1 oz.	Pear vinegar
1 tsp.	Dijon mustard
2 tsp.	Spice de Cosette seasoning
1 oz.	Mayonnaise
To taste	Kosher Salt & Pepper
4 oz.	Pecan Oil
2 oz.	Olive Oil

Method

Combine all ingredients in a blender.
Blend on high speed 2–3 minutes.

Salad

Ingredients

24 pieces	Shrimp, 21/25 count, peeled and deveined
8 oz.	Picked lump crabmeat
2 tbsp.	Pecans, chopped
2 tbsp.	Butter
24 pieces	Asparagus, trimmed
2	Red endive, cored and cleaned

Method

Melt butter in a hot sauté pan.

Add the shrimp, pecans, and crabmeat.

Sauté for 2–3 minutes; reserve and cool at room temperature.

Cut asparagus into bias pieces, about four pieces per asparagus spear.

Blanch in boiling well-salted water until firm but tender.

Cool rapidly with ice and pat dry.

Combine shrimp and crab mixture and asparagus and enough dressing to coat. Adjust seasoning.

Line individual plates or platters with endive leaves, coat with some dressing, and then portion the salad accordingly.

Garnish with some lemon slices and roasted pecans.

The Upside-Down Steward

The hierarchal order of a kitchen staff was very structured and important to those in it when I was starting out as an apprentice. Nowadays it does not seem proper that it was, and in some places remains, so rigid. In my kitchens today, I work to ensure that even though positions define everyone's role in the brigade hierarchy, everyone is seen as important and treated as such.

Some of the hardest-working people are the dishwashers and stewards (or porters). They make the least money and work extremely hard. They also play an instrumental role in food safety. Very clean dishes and utensils are a must to ensure good health and a high-operation.

The stewards empty garbage, wash pots, and do a job that many do not want to do. In fact, it comes as no surprise that many of these jobs are filled by minorities. I raise my toque (chef hat) to these stewards because without them and the important job they do day in and day out, we would be in trouble.

I ensure that the stewards in my kitchens are treated properly and fed well and that any person who works in or near the kitchen knows this. However, during my apprentice years, I did not always think this way.

One weekend at the catering house, we had five weddings in two days; it was a busy time for all. (Yes, this is the same catering house where I swam in gravy, if you are wondering—see the upcoming story "Into the Sauce.") At this time, I was in charge of basic prep as well as the sauces, soups, and stocks. This meant I had to have plenty of onions, potatoes, carrots, and other items peeled, cleaned, and sometimes cut for the cooks and chefs to use.

There were some new apprentices who would assist in the dicing, chopping, and special cuts needed for the weekend functions. Most of the time, however, the stewards, when they had downtime, were responsible for ensuring that all vegetables had been peeled, scraps were separated for stocks, and all vegetable products were put in the proper place.

The weekend prep started on Thursday, and the chef was in no mood to be played with. You could tell he was in a foul mood when a serious growl formed on his face and the hello you received was a type of "humph," rather than a cheerful "Hello, how are you today?" He called us in for our chefs' table meeting for comments, checklists, and at times, if you dared, feedback.

The cuisine had to be the best. He barked, "All of you need to pay attention and be the best you can this weekend. Five weddings means five married couples who will think they are on their honeymoon just by eating our food. That means more than 1,800 guests will think they are in gastronomic heaven because of my cuisine, my food."

I then made a mistake and said, "Chef, don't you think most people come to dance, drink, and enjoy a nice meal with lots of fun? The escoffier thing may be a bit too much, no?"

His face turned beet red. I thought his hat was going to blow off his head, and the others sank from the table as if to say, "Good luck; you are on your own."

I then received a lecture on cooking, being the best, and a chef's reputation. He said that unfortunately he had to depend on shoemakers such as me understanding good cuisine to make him look good. He went on to explain to me the importance of making whatever you cook the best, whether it is a classical dish under glass for a gourmet party, a simple hamburger, or a prime rib dinner. That is what will separate a great cook from a good cook and a good cook from a shoemaker.

Shoemaker. It did not seem like such a bad idea right now.

After the chef dismissed us from the meeting, I went to work. I was getting the crew ready. Stocks were simmering, sauces where in the making, and I had the stewards peeling and cleaning vegetables for us to use for the weekend. I left to help the cooks carve some pineapple boats for a first course and make the popover batter for the Yorkshire pudding that was going with the prime rib.

It seemed like we would never be done preparing food for 1,800! Each wedding had a different menu—there were so many items to prep and prepare! One wedding was even having a Baked Alaska Grand Success for its dessert in addition to the usual wedding cake.

I had to produce a Newburg sauce for the seafood, a beef sauce for the filet mignon, and an au jus for the prime rib. Most important, the stock for the chef's Chicken Consommé Stella and his famous tomato sauce both had to be perfect. The consommé was his own concoction, named after his daughter, and if it was not right, oh man, watch out.

I went back to the prep area and then to the kettles (which I finally did learn to work properly), and to my surprise and disbelief, I found onion peels, carrot peels, and tomato ends in my chicken stock. I was fuming. If the chef saw this and knew it was for his consommé, I would be in big trouble again.

Mind you, getting into trouble was a common occurrence during my training, but I'd be damned if some other person was going to do it for me! Trouble with the chef was one thing I needed no help in.

I quickly got a garbage can and removed the peels and other garbage from my simmering stock of chicken and proper vegetables. I then went to the stewards to get to the bottom of this culinary disaster. At first they claimed innocence. Then one of them said, "What is the big deal? What makes you think the stock is so good? Perhaps those vegetables will help it some." They started to laugh. I started to get mad and thought I was the chef, yelling and calling them shoemakers of the highest level!

Then one steward said "You are not the chef, and the way you cook perhaps you will never be, so leave us alone and next time I will check with you before I put the vegetable scraps in the stock, Mr. Chef Want-To-Be."

How dare he! Did he not know the ranking of the kitchen? Did he not know that I was a lead apprentice and he just a steward? I started to say things in languages that I did not know I knew, and I told him, "You are nothing but a steward. You know nothing about the food except cleaning it off a plate."

He said, "Well, I quit. Good bye, and you tell the chef why."

Then I said, "You are going nowhere." I grabbed him and lifted him up. All the apprentices and some of the cooks were watching as the chef came running down the hall toward all the commotion. I threw the steward in the garbage can with his legs sticking up and said, "Now enjoy my newest dish—Steward Upside-Down Cake."

I showed him. Then I looked up. Not one person was laughing. Had I not shown this steward? Had I not set an example for the stewards not to mess with us? Just then I saw the chef, and this time I think I went too far. A stream of Italian words came from him, and he called me into the office with the steward. After hearing everything, he told the steward to go for the day; the chef would call him and decide what to do. He then looked at me and shook his head with disappointment.

Although he understood the error in the stock and why I was upset, he did not understand the actions that I took. He did not understand the thoughtlessness of physically harming a person.

The chef said he had no choice but to let me go because if he did the not, the rest of the staff would think they could do such things. He asked how I would like it if for every mistake I made he took physical and verbal action in front of everybody.

It was a sad moment for me and for Chef. I was ruining the chance to learn and grow. I pleaded with him to give me one more chance. He said he would on the condition that he could show the staff that there is punishment for such behavior.

So, I spent the weekend washing dishes and emptying garbage with the other stewards instead of making sauces and helping put out great food for five weddings. It was my punishment. (The steward was taken off prep and placed on pot duty for two weeks for his actions.) I also had to apologize to the entire kitchen and really work hard to get back what little respect I had earned as an apprentice.

I wish that I had followed the Golden Rule, and I wish that my pride about my position in the kitchen had not overshadowed the person I really was. That is why we study management and supervision today. You cannot treat people in that manner, nor does anyone deserve such treatment.

The upside-down steward taught me a lot that weekend. He and I became good colleagues, and within two months he was an apprentice in the chef's kitchen doing vegetable preparation. I always tried to help him has much as possible, and I have learned to be fair and deal with difficult situations in a much better manner than I did that day.

Asparagus Salad in the French Way
with Asparagus Vinaigrette
(8 servings)

Ingredients

50	Asparagus spears, medium sized, with 1/2 inch trimmed off
1	Shallot, peeled and finely minced
2 oz.	Champagne vinegar
6	White imported anchovy fillets, minced
2 tbsp.	Parsley
8	Tarragon leaves
1 tbsp.	Lime zest, fine
6 oz.	Extra virgin olive oil
To taste	Kosher salt
To taste	Black pepper, freshly ground
4	Medium boiled eggs, peeled and pushed through a sieve or chopped fine
1/2 cup	Shaved Parmesan Reggiano cheese
2 tbsp.	Balsamic vinegar
2 tbsp.	Extra virgin olive oil

Method

Bring a 6- to 8-quart stockpot or saucepan of salted water to a boil.
Blanch asparagus spears 3–4 minutes, until tender but firm.
In a stainless steel bowl, combine the minced shallots and vinegar.
Stir to combine and let sit for 15 minutes.
In a food processor, combine anchovies, 10 of the asparagus spears, tarragon, parsley, lime zest, and 1 oz. of the oil and pulse for 2–3 minutes.
Whisk in remaining oil, then add vinegar and season with salt and pepper.
Arrange 5 asparagus spears each on plate, tips facing one way.
Place 1 oz. of dressing over each plate of asparagus.
Garnish with chopped hardboiled egg and cheese.
Drizzle with aged balsamic vinegar and extra virgin olive oil.

Penne alla Insalata with Plum Tomatoes and Red Onion Salad and Roasted Peppers with Ricotta Insalata
(4 servings)

Ingredients

8 oz.	Baby penne pasta
5	Roma plum tomatoes cut in quarters, seeded, and peeled
16	Black olives, pitted
1	Red onion, sliced thin (half moon)
2	Roasted peppers, thin strips
6 oz.	Extra virgin olive oil
2 oz.	25-year-old red wine vinegar
2 tsp.	Fresh basil or thyme
1/2 tsp.	Oregano
	Juice of one lemon
To taste	Salt and pepper
For garnish	Shaved insalata ricotta

Method

Combine all ingredients except cheese.

Toss gently, let stand 15 minutes, then go to next step.

Start cooking pasta in plenty of salted water.

When al dente, drain very well and immediately toss with the other ingredients.

Serve in individual bowls or one large one, topping the warm salad with ricotta shavings.

Ratatouille Salad
(4 servings)

Ingredients

1	Eggplant, cubed
5 tbsp.	Olive oil
1	Zucchini, cubed
1	Garlic clove, mashed
1	Red bell pepper, roasted, peeled, seeded, and cubed
1	Green bell pepper, roasted, peeled, seeded, and cubed
2 tbsp.	Regina® white wine vinegar
2 tbsp.	Ketchup
1 oz.	Fresh basil, finely chopped
To taste	Salt
4	Boston lettuce leaves

Method

Slightly salt the eggplant, let stand for 5–10 minutes, drain, and squeeze dry.

Heat 1 tbsp. olive oil in large skillet over high heat and sauté eggplant 2–3 minutes.

Add zucchini and garlic and sauté 2 minutes.

Reduce heat to medium.

Add red and green peppers and cook for 10 minutes.

Remove and place on an oiled sheet pan. Chill.

Using a stick blender, whip the vinegars, salt to taste, ketchup, and remaining olive oil in a large bowl. Add ratatouille mixture and toss with basil.

Let stand for 15 minutes, and then spoon over lettuce leaves.

Marinated Mushroom Salad
(4–6 servings)

Ingredients

1 lb.	Crimini or shitake mushrooms, stems removed
1 lb.	White button mushrooms, brushed clean
5 oz.	White onion, finely sliced
2 cloves	Garlic, sliced thin
3 oz.	Olive oil
2 oz.	12-year-aged balsamic vinegar
3 oz.	High-quality chicken stock
2	Bay leaves
2 tbsp.	Fresh tarragon, minced
1 tsp.	Mustard seed (optional)
1 oz.	Fresh chives, cut short
To taste	Kosher salt and fresh cracked white pepper

Method

In a medium saucepan, heat olive oil.

Add onions and sauté until translucent.

Add garlic and sauté 2 minutes more.

Add mushrooms and cook gently for 5 minutes, stirring often.

Add chicken stock, balsamic vinegar, bay leaf, rosemary, and mustard seed.

Bring to a boil.

Reduce heat and simmer for 10–12 minutes.

Pour mushrooms and liquids into stainless steel bowl, cover with plastic wrap, and refrigerate for at least 2 hours.

Prior to serving, sprinkle with chives to taste and toss with 2 tbsp. extra virgin olive oil.

Adjust seasoning with salt and pepper.

Crackling Shrimp Salad
with Oriental BBQ Dressing
(4 servings)

The Salad

Ingredients

1 lb.	Popcorn shrimp (in frozen food section)
	Note: You may purchase 21/25 count shrimp peeled and deveined and bread them yourself
1 cup	Button mushrooms, sliced
1	White onion, slivered
3 tbsp.	Peanut oil
4 tbsp.	Aged red wine vinegar
1 tsp.	Granulated garlic
2	Plum tomatoes, halved and seeded
1 cup	Broccoli florets
2 cups	Salad greens
2 cups	BBQ dressing (see following recipe)

Method

Deep fry shrimp until golden brown.

Remove and drain on paper towels.

In skillet, sauté mushrooms and onions in oil for 1–2 minutes.

Add vinegar, sautéing until mushrooms and onions are slightly tender, 2–3 minutes more.

Blanch broccoli in salted boiling water. Drain and cool.

Toss salad greens and broccoli with 1/2 cup of dressing.

Place in bowls and top with tomatoes, mushrooms, and onions.

Toss shrimp with another 1/2 cup of dressing and distribute over the salads evenly.

BBQ Oriental Dressing

Ingredients

¹/₂ cup	Your favorite BBQ sauce
¹/₄ cup	Mushroom soy sauce
¹/₂ cup	Oyster sauce
3 oz.	Sesame seed oil
2 cups	Chicken broth
1 cup	Rice wine vinegar
2 tbsp.	Ground ginger
¹/₂ cup	Scallions, chopped

Method

In large jar or bowl, mix all ingredients well, or place in blender and pulse for 30 seconds.

Summer Potato Salad
(4–6 servings)

Ingredients

1 lb.	Yukon potatoes, diced
3 oz.	Bacon, diced
2	Shallots, diced
1/2 cup	Celery, diced
1/2 cup	Mayonnaise
1/2 cup	Extra virgin olive oil
1 tbsp.	Dijon mustard
2 tbsp.	White wine vinegar
1–1 1/2 tsp.	Worcestershire sauce
1 tsp.	Tarragon, minced
To taste	Kosher salt and pepper
6	Medium hardboiled eggs
1 tbsp.	Parsley, chopped
1 head	Romaine lettuce

Method

Put potatoes in cold water.
Bring to a boil and simmer until tender but still firm.
Dry.
In a sauté pan, fry bacon.
Add onions and cook until tender.
Add celery to potatoes.
In a large bowl, combine all other ingredients except eggs to make the dressing.
Combine potatoes and 4 of the eggs with the dressing.
Serve over a bed of cleaned Romaine lettuce and garnish with chopped parsley and some slices of the two reserved eggs.

Soup's On

*A*fter endless hours of peeling, dicing, slicing, and knife cuts, I was getting a chance to cook for the lunch shift. It was a big step to start working behind the line with the sous-chef and his crew. The menu ranged from sandwiches and nice salads to hot main plates and fresh-made soups that the chef took the utmost pride in. He was recognized at the club for producing some great soups, and he taught me that you can tell a good cook by his or her soup.

Chef said soups may seem simple, but the craft of making a flavorful one with the right consistency and balance of flavors is difficult. He also said a great soup, fresh bread, and a nice salad can make a great meal, especially on a cold day.

In classical cuisine, soups were served to start off the most elegant dinners. These soups were clear, flavorful consommés or perhaps elegant lobster bisques. While I was taught all this, at the end of the day it was just soup to me, and I thought the chef was a little too stressed about it. To me, the main plates, the salads with decorations, and food from the stove were the exciting stuff. How hard could this soup thing be?

The next day I was to get the entire prep, or *mis en place* (a French term for "everything in its place"), ready for the day's selection of soup. The chef was going to come in and put it all together and show me the finished product. We worked on the stove step by step making these two soups; he was very strict about every step, ensuring that things were correct.

One soup was fish chowder and the other a roasted beef and onion soup with beef broth. I was under pressure; the chef was barking orders to the whole line as service time drew near. I was told to add the broths to the soups now because the vegetables and other items were ready, and to *move it*. Chef said, "You move so slow—this is for today's lunch, not tomorrow's."

Well, I did what I was told and added the broths and set the soups to simmer. Lunch started, and it was a busy day. As I did more prep and assisted the pantry chef, I noticed that many of the cups of soup came back to the dishwasher almost full.

Then I saw the dining room captain speaking with the chef; it did not look good.

The chef came back into the kitchen with a very red face and steam coming from his ears. "Leonard, over here NOW!" he yelled. I stood at the stove near the two pots of soup as the chef tasted them. He then made me taste both soups, and I believe he wanted to place me in the stockpot with them.

It turned out that I added the fish broth to the onion soup and the beef broth to the fish chowder, none of which went over well with the club members. If the members of the club were unhappy with this, I realized that Chef was livid. I received a big lecture about focus, concentration, tasting all items before they leave the kitchen, and basically knowing what the heck you are doing. But that was not all. I had to eat two bowls of each soup and drink two cups of each broth to learn the difference between fish and beef broth (I really do know now) to suffer the agony of my mistake.

Once again I left for the day wondering whether they needed any help at the local carwash and hoping to find something to settle my upset stomach. I did learn a few things that day, however. I learned that it is not just soup. I also learned that fish chowder made with beef broth is not very good, and the same can be said for roasted beef soup made with fish broth.

New England-Style Clam Chowder
(8 servings)

Ingredients

10 each	Cherrystone clams, washed
1 cup	Water
2 oz.	Salt pork, minced to a paste
2 oz.	Onions, minced
2 oz.	Celery, finely diced
2 oz.	Flour
6 oz.	Potatoes, diced small
1/2 qt.	Milk, scalded
2/3 cup	Heavy cream, scalded
To taste	Salt
To taste	White pepper
To taste	Tabasco sauce
To taste	Worcestershire sauce

Method

Steam the clams in water in a covered pot until they open.
Strain the broth through a filter or cheesecloth and reserve it.
Pick, chop, and reserve the clams.
Render the salt pork in the soup pot.
Add the onions and celery and sweat until they are translucent.
Add the flour and cook to make a roux.
Add reserved broth and milk gradually and incorporate it completely, working out any lumps that might form.
Simmer for 30 minutes, skimming the surface as necessary.
Add the potatoes to the soup and simmer until tender.
Add the reserved clams and cream.
Adjust the seasoning to taste with salt, white pepper, Tabasco, and Worcestershire sauce.

Roasted Eggplant Soup
(8 servings)

Ingredients

1 large	Eggplant
2 cloves	Garlic, sliced thin
3 cups	High-quality chicken stock
1 small	Onion, diced small
1 medium	Carrot, diced small
2 ribs	Celery, diced small
4 tbsp.	Extra virgin olive oil
4 oz.	Butter
To taste	Kosher salt
To taste	Black pepper

Method

Preheat oven to 350°. Cut eggplant in half. Rub lightly with olive oil and season well with salt and pepper. Place on baking sheet and roast in the oven for approximately 30 minutes, or until the eggplant becomes very soft.

In a large soup pot, heat 3 tbsp. of olive oil. Sauté the carrots, onions, celery, and half of the garlic. Continue to cook the vegetables until they become lightly caramelized.

When the eggplant is fully cooked, remove from the oven and allow to cool long enough so that it can be handled. Once it has cooled, scrape all of the meat out of the inside of the eggplant.

Add the eggplant to the soup pot along with 2 cups of the chicken broth and bring to a simmer.

Purée the soup in a blender and season with salt and pepper.

Use the remaining chicken stock to adjust the thickness of the soup.

Take the remaining garlic and fry lightly in olive oil until crispy. This may be used as garnish for the soup.

Ounce the soup is smooth, finish it with the diced cold butter and adjust the seasoning with salt and pepper.

Pasta and Bean Soup
(6–8 servings)

Ingredients

12 oz.	Dried white beans, soaked overnight
2 oz.	Pancetta, diced small
4 oz.	Olive oil
2 oz.	Butter
1 small	Onion, diced small
1 rib	Celery, diced small
2	Carrots, diced small
3 oz.	Tomato paste
2 oz.	High-quality red wine
1 qt.	High-quality chicken stock
6 oz.	Parmesan rind
3 cloves	Garlic, sliced thin
2 sprigs	Fresh rosemary
3 leaves	Fresh sage, rough chopped
To taste	Kosher salt
To taste	Freshly ground black pepper
4 oz.	Cooked petite penne pasta or other small pasta
2 tbsp.	Extra virgin olive oil
2 tbsp.	Butter, diced

Method

Heat olive oil and butter in a large soup pot over medium heat.
Sauté the pancetta, garlic, onions, carrots, and celery until lightly caramelized.
Add tomato paste and mix well. Continue stirring while cooking tomato paste for 3–5 minutes.
Deglaze with red wine. Allow the wine to reduce by half.
Add the beans and Parmesan rind to the pot along with rosemary and sage.
Add the chicken stock and bring to a boil. Lower heat to a simmer and cook for 2–3 hours, stirring occasionally, until beans are tender.
Remove the Parmesan rind and discard. Remove half of the beans with liquid and purée in a blender or food processor. Add the purée back to the soup and mix well.
Season with salt and pepper, add pasta, butter, and olive oil, and serve.

Chicken and Dumpling Soup
(6 servings)

Ingredients

1/2 cup	Mushrooms
2 ribs	Celery, diced small
2	Carrots, diced small
1/2 cup	Sweet onion, diced small
2 oz.	Butter
2 oz.	Duck fat or chicken fat
2 oz.	Flour
4 cups	Double chicken stock or high-quality chicken broth
1/2 cup	Roasted chicken meat, diced medium
1/2 cup	English peas
1 tsp.	Fresh thyme, finely chopped
To taste	Kosher salt
To taste	Freshly cracked black pepper
1 recipe	Dumpling dough

Method

In a large saucepan, cook onions, celery, carrots, and mushrooms in the butter until tender.

Add flour and cook 2–3 minutes.

Stir in chicken broth and allow to simmer for 5 minutes.

Stir in cooked chicken and fresh thyme. Add kosher salt and pepper to taste.

Drop dumpling dough from a small spoon onto top of soup and bring to a boil.

Allow to cook until the dumplings are cooked all the way through, approximately 10 minutes.

Add peas right before serving.

Adjust seasoning and serve.

Roasted Butternut Squash Soup with Chestnuts
(6 servings)

Ingredients

2 each	Butternut squash, peeled and seeded
As needed	Extra virgin olive oil
4 oz.	Butter
1 small	Onion, diced small
2 small	Carrots, diced small
2 ribs	Celery, diced small
1 cup	Chestnuts, peeled and sliced
1 qt.	High-quality chicken stock
4 oz.	Honey
1 tbsp.	Cinnamon
1/2 pt.	Heavy cream

Method

Preheat oven to 300°. Cut the squash into a medium dice. Lightly coat with olive oil and place onto a baking sheet. Season lightly with salt and pepper. Continue to roast until the squash is very soft, approximately 45 minutes.

In a large soup pot, heat 3 tbsp. of olive oil and sauté the carrots, onion, and celery until lightly caramelized.

Add the chicken stock and one-half the chestnuts and simmer for 10 minutes, stirring occasionally.

When the squash is soft, add it to the soup pot and simmer for a few more minutes.

Purée the soup in a blender until it is nice and smooth.

Add the cinnamon, honey, heavy cream, and butter.

Adjust the seasoning with salt and pepper.

Adjust the consistency, if needed, with some hot milk or broth.

Garnish soup with remaining chestnuts.

Never on a Boat

*W*hen you are an apprentice, you never know what will be requested of you. In most cases it involves doing what others do not want to do, including mundane work that the cooks and chefs no longer do as they rise through the ranks.

I remember the day the chef came to me and said, "We have a situation here. One of the top members of the club needs to have food on his boat for a trip to New York and back. He also wants a cook on board to take care of the meal. It will be for six to eight people, so even an apprentice should be able to handle it."

I was not quite sure, but I did not think that the chef was giving a compliment.

He told me the hour to be at the boat and said this would be a good test to see how far I had come and how much I had learned. This was my big chance to impress the chef, a member of the club, and his guests. Surely once I did a great job word would get back to the chef and I would be in his good graces and perhaps be moved up through the ranks. I was going to rock the boat, so to speak.

I studied a few books and wrote a very impressive menu that was sure to get me to the chefs' promised land. The first course would be a nice consommé of chicken, the second would be pan-seared tournedos of beef finished au poivre style, and dessert would be a masterpiece Grand Marnier soufflé with vanilla sauce and marinated oranges. Oh, man, these guests would have the lunch of lunches on their excursion to New York.

The morning of the trip came, and I woke very early to pack my prep and make sure I had all the food and utensils I needed. I thought the chef would be up and in the kitchen to check on me, but the sous-chef said that sometimes Chef will just let you swim to see if you are going to drown or not. That was great to hear. I thought, "Well, I will show the sous-chef and the chef. They will see what a fine cook this apprentice can be."

I got on the boat and met the captain in charge along with the butler who would be serving my meal. They gave me a tour and then showed me the galley, making it clear that I was to stay in that area. A bathroom and shower were below for the staff, and the guests were not to be interrupted by the help.

A bit snobby I thought. I bet they wouldn't speak to Chef like this. But I did not worry. Once they dined on my food, they would ask to meet this aspiring chef.

I started to set up in the kitchen and noticed a few things. One was the very limited space: a small stove with only two burners and a griddle, an oven that was a bit small, and a limited number of pots and pans. I also noticed that all of the equipment was electric.

Well, I went to work as the boat started to shove off. I could hear the guests laughing and getting settled above me. The view from the galley was great, and there I was, about to cook a full meal for guests on a yacht and have a great day touring the ocean as well. What a life! Perhaps one day I would be a chef for the wealthy on their yachts or in their huge homes. Who knew?

I started the soup first, mixing in the items for the raft to make the soup crystal clear and flavorful. It was on the stove with the heat turned up just a bit to get it to a boil. The key to a good consommé is to let the raft simmer once it has reached a boil so it does not break. The proteins in the ingredients make the raft solid and then clarify any impurities and infuse the stock with flavor. If the raft should break, the stock will be cloudy and unpleasing to the eye.

As the soup simmered, I started to prep the meat and the vegetables along with the items for the soufflé. The butler wiped the china and polished the silverware for the party upstairs, hardly saying a word to me. "All business," I thought. "This world of catering to people is serious stuff, I guess."

The lunch was to be served in about two hours, when the boat circled the Statue of Liberty and they all could enjoy a meal and the view. The soup was simmering fine, and everything was ready to cook with 30 minutes to start time. All of a sudden the boat started to rock as we hit some rough waters entering the New York Harbor area. It went a bit back and forth, which did not do wonders for my already nervous stomach.

As the boat rocked some more, I noticed the consommé was rocking as well. It rocked so hard that the raft broke and the consommé kept swishing back and forth, spilling out of the pot. I tried to grab the pot and take it off the stove, but it was too late. The raft had broken, and it was mixed in with the stock that was to be served clear as a piece of glass.

The butler came and said, "I hope you are ready. I will pick up the first course in 10 minutes."

I did my best to strain the consommé, but it was cloudy and had fat in it. It looked a bit like the chicken noodle soup we serve the staff at the club for family meals. I garnished the bowls, brought the now-dirty consommé to a boil, and flavored it with some herbs, salt, and a bit of butter. The butler came to pick it up. He looked at the bowls and in the soup terrine and said, "What, may I ask, is this?" with a very condescending look.

I said nervously, "It is a buttery chicken broth with vegetables."

"Oh," he said. "That's funny, I thought you said consommé earlier."

As the butler left, I started to get the meat ready to sear. The stove, however, had its limits, and the cast iron pan I brought with me was not getting very hot. I knew they wanted the next course soon, so I placed the meat in the pan and heard a faint sizzle. After three minutes, I turned the steaks over to see steamed meat rather than a great golden brown color of seared beef. I quickly blasted the oven as hot as I could and placed the steaks in the oven. I started to heat the vegetables, the sauce, and potatoes.

It was time for the next course. As I opened the oven door, smoke billowed out into my face. I dropped the pan with the steaks, and the whole galley filled with smoke. The butler hastily opened the windows and the door. I heard a yell from upstairs: "Is everything fine down there?"

I picked up the steaks, brushed them off, and placed them in the hot pan. Then I placed the vegetables on the plate with the potatoes and put the meat beside them on a toasted Holland Rusk of bread. Next I had to make the pepper sauce, but to flame the brandy would be hard with an electric stove rather than gas, so I placed a match near the edge of the pan as I poured the brandy. This was not a good idea. The brandy caught the flame from the pan and spread to the bottle, which was now on fire. I threw the bottle into the sink and covered it with wet towels and ice cubes.

The butler watched in amazement. I finished the sauce, topped the steaks with it, and drizzled some more on the plate. By now I was a wreck. The brandy fire died, and I had to get dessert ready.

I whipped the egg yolks, then I whipped the whites, folded everything together, and poured the mix into my buttered ramekins. I placed the ramekins on a tray and put them in the oven. (I was soon to learn another lesson of many that day.) I finished the dessert sauce, marinated the fruit, and was all set when I smelled something I shouldn't have been smelling. I had forgotten to lower the oven rack after the steaks. The soufflés had risen, but they were a rich dark brown on the outside and not really done on the inside.

What do I do now, I wondered! There's no time and no ingredients to make new ones, and these would either fall like deflated balloons or be black on the outside if I cooked them any longer.

The butler was coming as I lowered the oven to warm. He returned the plates. Most of the food was eaten. It could not have been so bad, I said to myself. "Good thing they are drinking so much," said the butler. "They cannot notice your bad food." I ignored that statement, even though I was tempted to throw him overboard.

I took the soufflés out of the oven, but as soon as I started to plate them they were falling. So I turned them upside down and served the sauce and fruit around the soufflé.

"Let me guess," said the butler, "warm orange cake with vanilla sauce."

"Exactly," I said, "and thanks for what you are doing." Even though he was obnoxious, I knew he was covering and felt bad for me.

Well, we were about 45 minutes from docking on the return trip, so I cleaned the galley and packed everything. When I was done, I sat outside the galley and looked at the ocean. "Well, let's see Mr. Smarty Chef Want-To-Be," I said.

Lesson One: Become familiar with the kitchen you are cooking in and the environment prior to writing a menu.

Lesson Two: Know what equipment you have available prior to writing a menu.

Lesson Three: Review the menu and plan and ask questions prior to attempting things you have never have done before.

Preparation is everything. That day I figured out that being properly prepared will ensure a better outcome of any venture you may undertake.

I returned to work the next day and started on my vegetable prep and lessons in sauce making. The sous-chef called out and said that the chef wanted to see me in his office. Oh boy, this was it. I sank; he had let me in the water and I had drowned.

He sat me down and said the club member had just gotten off the phone with him and the butler had just left his office. He gave me an envelope. Damn, my pink slip before I finished the apprenticeship.

I said, "Thanks for everything Chef." He looked at me puzzled and said, "What is wrong with you, Leonard?"

"This envelope—it means I am finished, no?" He looked at me as if I were crazy. "You are a piece of work," he said. "It is a $100 tip for yesterday. The butler dropped it off; he mentioned you had some challenges but said that you pulled through okay."

As I left the office, he said, "Never forget, not all will go perfect. Not now, not even 10 years from now when you have the title you want. What we learn, how we persevere, and the final result we manage to make happen regardless of the challenges is all that will really matter."

I left feeling a bit better, but mostly I took what I had learned the hard way as another step in my long journey.

Chef Victor's Avocado Crab Cakes
(8 first course servings; 4 main dish servings)

Ingredients

2 tbsp.	Oil
2 tbsp.	Butter
1/4 cup	Onion, diced fine
1/4 cup each	Red and yellow roasted peppers, diced small
2 tsp.	Fresh thyme leaf, picked and minced
1	Egg
1/2 cup	Mayonnaise
2/3 oz.	Worcestershire sauce
1/3 tsp.	Tabasco sauce
1/3 oz.	Dry mustard
1 tsp.	Whole grain mustard
1 tsp.	Spice de Cosette seasoning
1 tsp.	Giancarlo chili spice
2 tbsp.	Parsley, chopped
2 cups	Bread crumbs (made by removing crust and grating bread in food processor)
1	Avocado, diced
2 lbs.	Lump crabmeat, shell free
As needed	Canola oil

Method

Sauté onions and peppers lightly in oil and butter until translucent; let cool.

Combine the next 10 ingredients and one cup of the bread crumbs with the sautéed onions and peppers.

Gently fold in lump crabmeat and avocado.

Shape into 4-oz. cakes.

Dredge cakes in reserved fresh bread crumbs.

Sauté cakes in minimal amount of canola oil until golden brown and finish in 350° oven for 10–12 minutes.

Serve with your favorite salsa or tartar sauce.

Maryland She-Oyster Stew
(8 servings)

Ingredients

1 pt.	Fresh oysters, shucked
2 tbsp.	Olive oil
1 tbsp.	Butter
2 tbsp.	Shallots
3 oz.	White wine
2 cups	Light cream
2 cups	Heavy cream
2 tsp.	Salt
1 tsp.	Black pepper
2 tsp.	Hot sauce
2 tsp.	Chervil
2 tbsp.	Unsalted butter, cold

Method

Preheat a 2-quart saucepan.

Gently sauté shallots in olive oil and butter.

Add oysters and sauté until just plump; remove oysters from the pan.

Deglaze pan with white wine and reduce by half.

Add cream and simmer for 5 minutes.

Return oysters to pan and season with salt, pepper, and hot sauce.

Finish soup by swirling in fresh butter and chervil.

Crabmeat Omelet
(4 servings)

Ingredients

4	Plum tomatoes, quartered and seeded
2 oz.	Virgin olive oil
1 clove	Garlic, minced
16 oz.	Crabmeat, picked
1 tsp.	Basil, chopped
1/2 tsp.	Sage, chopped
1 tsp.	Spice de Cosette seasoning
2 oz.	Extra virgin olive oil
	Juice of 1 lime
6 oz.	Cooked rice
12	Eggs, beaten
4 oz.	Cream

Method

Toss tomatoes with oil and garlic.
Place in roasting pan on a rack and roast in 425° oven 3–5 minutes.
Reserve.
Whip eggs and cream together and mix well with crabmeat, basil, sage,
Spice de Cosette, extra virgin olive oil, lime juice, and cooked rice.
Make 4 individual omelets with 3 eggs and 1 oz. cream each.
Fill each omelet with 4 oz. of crab filling.
To serve, garnish with small basil leaves and fresh, clean lime wedges.
Top each omelet with four roasted tomato quarters.

New England Rice and Shrimp Fritters
(12 servings)

Batter

Ingredients

24 oz.	Flour
6 oz.	Eggs
1 oz.	Olive oil
1 oz.	Melted Butter
To taste	Old Bay seasoning
To taste	Salt
	Juice of 1 lime
12 oz.	Sparkling water

Method

Mix all items in a processor or blender.
Let sit for at least 4 hours.

Filling

Ingredients

2 oz.	Butter
4 oz.	Onions, diced small
4 oz.	Celery, diced small
12 oz.	Salad shrimp
10 oz.	Cooked rice

Method

Melt butter in pan.
Cook onions and celery until soft.
Add shrimp and rice.
Season, then cool.
Fold in all of the batter.
Spoon batter, about 2 oz. for each fritter, and fry at 350° to golden brown.
Serve with lemon and/or lime wedges and your favorite tartar sauce.

Chocolate Almond Pinwheels
(3 dozen)

Ingredients

1¹/₂ cups	Unsalted butter, softened
1¹/₂ cups	Brown sugar
3³/₄ cups	Flour
³/₄ tsp.	Salt
18 oz.	Milk chocolate chips
1¹/₂ cups	Sliced almonds, lightly toasted

Method

Cream butter and sugar together.

Blend in flour and salt until a smooth dough is formed.

Press the dough into a half sheet pan carefully and bake at 300° for approximately 15–20 minutes, or until golden brown (toothpick is left clean). Be careful not to overcook.

Remove from oven immediately and sprinkle with chocolate chips.

Let stand for 2 minutes; spread chips evenly over cookie base using either a spatula or a palette knife.

Sprinkle with almonds. Cut into triangles while still warm.

Allow to cool completely.

Remove from pan and serve.

Notes:

Although this recipe is extremely simple, care needs to be taken in preparation; otherwise, the dough will be tough or overcooked.

DO NOT, under any circumstances, grease the pan.

This dessert should be prepared using only milk chocolate, so that when it is finished it resembles a candy bar.

Cut into 3-inch squares (4 rows × 5 rows) or decrease size to approximately 2¹/₂-inch squares (5 rows × 6 rows), then cut each along the diagonal to create triangles.

Grape-Nuts® Custard Crunch
(12 servings)

Ingredients

6	Whole eggs
2	Egg yolks
³/₄ cup	Sugar
4 tbsp.	Dark brown sugar
1¹/₂ tbsp.	Pure vanilla extract
1 tbsp.	Cinnamon
1 qt.	Milk, scalded
1 cup	Light cream
1 cup	Grape-Nuts cereal

Garnish

Whipped cream, sweetened
Berries
Cinnamon or Grape-Nuts cereal
Chocolate curls (optional)

Method

Beat eggs, yolks, sugars, vanilla, and cinnamon together.
Gradually add scalded milk and the light cream.
Spray an 8 × 10 inch baking pan (2" deep) with vegetable oil spray.
Strain custard into pan through a fine strainer.
Sprinkle evenly with cereal.
Cover pan with foil and place in a larger pan. Add hot water until it reaches halfway up the sides of the custard pan.
Bake at 350° for 60 minutes.
Remove from water bath and allow to cool slightly before placing custard in refrigerator. Allow to set overnight.
To serve, cut into squares and garnish with lightly sweetened whipped cream, a few berries, and a sprinkle of Grape-Nuts, or a dust of cinnamon.

Reader's Notes and Thoughts

Into the Sauce

*I*was getting my second apprentice job as a saucier for a large catering house. This would be a good job with the chance to work on large banquets and do some exciting things with sauces and gravies. It would be an opportunity to start using the skills I had learned to date in my career.

The kitchen was big; it had soup kettles large enough to take a bath in, huge ovens that held many pans, and a battery of stoves that could cook for more than 1,000 people. The chef was Italian and very tough with his standards and expectations.

The first few weeks were going well; we were making some nice items, and the customer feedback on the food was very good. I prided myself on sauces for all of the dishes. The chef taught me how to make a tomato sauce that was just great—not quite Grandma's, but great.

Making a sauce that people want to lick off the plate is an art form; it is a craft. Most great chefs consider the saucier to be the second most important position (next to master chef, of course). A good sauce is the ultimate compliment to a dish; it brings the other food to life and creates a foundation on the plate that makes all other items so much better.

In the catering hall, we made all of our stocks and broths early in the week and then would make the gravies and sauces for the busy weekends. It was a Thursday I would never forget. I had five soup kettles going, all simmering with the aromatic smell of great sauces. These sauces would be the hit of the weekend; they would make the chicken sing, the fish start to swim, and the beef happy to be on a plate. Yes sir, my sauces would ensure that the party was a success.

As the sauces were simmering I tried adjusting the steam controls just right. This was a challenge at times because the old kettles worked off a steam pipe control and it was a matter of manually making the right adjustment to ensure that you got the heat distribution you wanted.

The executive chef came by, and we started discussing the events for the weekend and some of the great things we were starting to do. I stood there feeling proud and thinking, "This is what it is all about—the chef watching me, the apprentice, make his food come alive with great sauces." Just then Chef looked over and said, "I think you have a problem here." I quickly turned around and saw that my kettle adjustments were not done correctly. The heat was too high, and three of the five kettles were now overflowing with bubbling sauces.

I reacted very quickly and ran with a towel to adjust the settings and turn down the kettles. Like an Olympic athlete, I would gracefully cross the floor of sauce and put a stop to this. One problem. I am not an Olympic athlete. As I ran, the floor of gravy pulled out beneath me and down I went. Chef looked on as I took a ride down the kitchen line on my gravy-covered behind and slammed into the wall at the end of the kitchen. The staff came running to help shut down the kettles, and Chef was asking, "Are you okay?"

I was, outside of some embarrassment and soreness.

The next day I came to work, and there was a sign on the kitchen wall. It read: "To Our New Apprentice of the Sauces. He Really Falls for His Work."

To this day, the one consistent principle for apprentices and master chefs alike is that just when you are feeling good about things and starting to get into that cloud, something will happen to bring you down to earth!

Creole Honey Mustard Sauce

Ingredients

2	Shallots, minced
3 cloves	Garlic, minced
3 tbsp.	Olive oil
3/4 cup	Red wine
2 oz.	Dijon or creole mustard
1/2 cup	Roasted peppers, diced fine
3 oz.	Franks red hot sauce
1 tbsp.	Cajon spice
1 cup	Mayonnaise
1 cup	Sour cream
2 tbsp.	Honey
To taste	Kosher salt
To taste	Cayenne pepper

Method

Sweat shallots and garlic in oil.
Deglaze pan with wine; reduce 2–3 minutes.
Blend all remaining ingredients well.

Chef's Walnut Pesto

Ingredients

4 slices	White bread, crust removed, soaked in milk
5 cloves	Garlic, crushed
1 cup	Walnuts, toasted
1 cup	Basil leaves
1–2 cups	Extra virgin olive oil
1¹/₂ cups	Fresh ricotta
¹/₂ cup	Reggiano, grated

Method

Place all ingredients except extra virgin olive oil in food processor.
Pulse, then start drizzling olive oil while pulsing. Use 1 cup of olive oil
first. Check consistency, then add more, 2 tbsp. at at time, if needed, until
a nice sauce consistency is obtained without being oily.
Toss with hot pasta or use with salads as a dressing.

Red Currant Sauce

Ingredients

3 oz.	Butter
2 tbsp.	Oil
2 oz.	Bacon, diced small
1 small	Onion, diced small
1/2 cup	Carrots, diced small
3 cloves	Garlic, minced
3 tbsp.	Flour
2	Bay leaves
6 stems	Parsley
2 sprigs	Fresh thyme
2 tsp.	Peppercorns, crushed
2 oz.	White wine vinegar
5 oz.	Red wine
2 cups	Demi-glace
1 cup	Venison stock or beef broth
1 cup	Red currants or red currant jelly with currants
3 oz.	Cold butter, diced, for finishing

Method

Heat butter and oil; render bacon; add carrots, onion, and garlic.
Sauté until soft; add flour and cook.
Add spices, herbs, vinegar, and wine; mix well.
Reduce to half.
Add 2 cups demi-glace and 1 cup venison stock.
Simmer 20–30 minutes; strain well.
Fold in 3 oz. cold butter and 1 cup cooked red currants or red current jelly with currants.

Prosciutto Sauce

Ingredients

1 cup	Chicken broth
1 cup	Tomato sauce
4 oz.	Tomato, diced
1/2 cup	Prosciutto, diced fine
2 tbsp.	Butter
1 cup	Hot milk
1/2 tsp.	Pepper, freshly ground
1/2 cup	Parmesan cheese, grated

Method

Place chicken broth, tomato sauce, and diced tomato in saucepot and simmer for 30–40 minutes.

Sauté prosciutto in butter on low heat until fat is cooked out.

Add pepper, then hot milk.

Stir with wooden spoon until all the milk has just about cooked out and evaporated.

Add cheese.

Add tomato and broth mixture and simmer for 20 minutes.

Adjust seasoning.

Tomato Garlic Sauce

Ingredients

3 oz.	Extra virgin olive oil
1/2 medium	Onion, diced
5 cloves	Garlic, sliced
2 tbsp.	Tomato paste
2 1/2 cups	Tomatoes, diced
1/2 cup	Red wine
1 tsp.	Sage, minced
1 tbsp.	Basil, minced
1 tbsp.	Roasted granulated garlic or roasted garlic purée
1 cup	Seafood or chicken broth
2 tbsp.	Butter
2 tbsp.	Extra virgin olive oil

Method

Heat 3 oz. oil and sauté onions and garlic until tender, then add tomato paste.

Cook 1–2 minutes.

Add tomatoes and sauté 3–4 minutes more.

Deglaze with red wine.

Add herbs and granulated garlic or garlic purée.

Finish with broth, butter, and 2 tbsp. oil.

Simmer for 5–10 minutes.

Adjust seasoning.

Sushi Before Its Time

*I*n the culinary world, there are many cooking and exhibit competitions around the country. Although the public is not aware of many of these, in the industry they are very popular, and they serve as a way for apprentices and chefs to develop their skills. Most shows and competitions are held at industry trade shows or culinary events. They range from hot food competitions, where cooks and chefs prepare dishes within a time limit under a judge's watchful eye, to the buffet program, which consists of platters of displayed food that show the skills of the cold kitchen.

In my early days as an apprentice, I watched chefs compete in these shows as they displayed awesome platters of meat or fish with intricate garnishes and even truffle paintings and sculptures.

Well, the day came for my first show. It was being held in conjunction with a restaurant show. I decided to do a fish platter and really thought hard to come up with something different and new. My chef, though helpful, said, "This one is on your own; you need to make mistakes to learn, and I want to see what you can do." As I look back now, after being a seasoned competitor for the past 24 years, I cannot help but wonder what planet I was on with this fish platter.

All displays in those days where done on silver trays, and the trays were coated with a coat of aspic or gelatin. This was done mostly to protect the silver tray when a customer took food off the platter with a utensil. Classically, the gelatin was made from the bones of the product you were displaying—meat, fish, poultry, and such. The food also got brushed or glazed with this jelly to help keep it fresh looking and protect it for the time it was out. Again, in classical times, real jellies were made, and a serving of food would receive a light coat for flavor and freshness.

I created a salmon platter for this competition with a roulade of stuffed salmon; a gravlax and garnishes of cucumber cups filled with chopped eggs, capers, and red onions; and pastry cups filled with a shrimp mousse. I glazed some thin, raw slices of salmon and placed them on a rice cup, topping them with caviar. Man, was I cooking—or so I thought.

We had some very small sardines in the house, and that gave me another idea.

Not all ideas are good, as I would learn. I decided to pour the gelatin on my platter and then I would set these small sardines in spots on the platter to create the effect of fish swimming in water. Once the gelatin set, I would display the salmon and garnishes on top. I even went so far as to add a touch of blue food color to the gelatin for a true ocean effect!

How proud I was of that platter. It had this great sliced salmon with all the garnishes and a display of the gravlax, all presented on a water view with small fish swimming upstream.

The chef and the cooks in the kitchen gave me a very odd look and then went to huddle and discuss something. I heard some chuckles and figured they were jealous that they did not think of this. I took my platter to the show, checked in, and placed it on my assigned spot on the table. I was in awe of many of the platters and unbelievable cakes and pastries, as well as the other chefs busy placing the final touches on their work.

I went home and got some sleep before the judging began. When I returned, the judging was still not done, so I walked through the trade show and saw new food products and met some good people in the industry. Finally the doors to the culinary salon opened. I rushed in and saw all the displays, many with ribbons for gold, silver, and bronze medals and special awards. I went to the table with the seafood platters and saw some nice displays with awards. When I got to my platter, there was no award.

My heart sank. All that hard work, creativity, and effort put into my first platter and not even an honorable mention. This was not right! It was an injustice in the culinary world! Perhaps the chef set this up to teach me.

The judges then came around to give critiques to those who wanted some feedback. They introduced themselves and then gave a very long, hard look at my work. They commented on how nice the salmon and my garnishes were and then proceeded to beat me up about the gravlax, the raw salmon, and then the big one: the blue gelatin with the fish inside.

I learned very quickly that blue was not a natural food color and should never be used in a show and that you cannot make blue fish stock to make blue gelatin. One judge said the real letdown was the swimming fish. What was I thinking, little fish uncooked in a platter with raw salmon and caviar? He thought about having it removed from the show. He said that this was against all culinary process and very wrong. He asked, "What were you thinking? Do you think you are in Japan—raw fish, sushi? Americans do not eat this. You need to go back to good classical fundamentals."

"It was nice to meet you too, Chef," I thought to myself. After the beating, I reflected and learned many things. First, many of the judges and other chefs at the show would play a role in my culinary career as I entered more shows and started to climb the ladder to chefdom. Second, a chef should never use blue food color. Third, sushi was something Americans would come to consume and enjoy, but it wasn't time yet. And finally, as a very young lad, a mere apprentice in the field of cookery, I was presenting sushi before its time. Oh, what could have been!

Creative ideas and concepts may not always fit the first time or apply to what you are working on, but they still may be good ideas and should never be discarded. Cook, create, and follow your heart, and your ideas for food may make a splash one day!

Red Snapper with Shrimp
and Potato Hash
(6 servings)

Red Snapper

Ingredients

6 6-oz. portions	Red snapper filet
3 oz.	Olive oil
2 oz.	Honey
1 tsp.	Kosher salt
4 tbsp.	Fresh lime juice
2 tbsp.	Butter
3 tbsp.	Olive oil
3 oz.	Fresh lemon juice
2 oz.	White wine
6 oz.	Cold butter, diced
1 tsp.	Parsley, chopped
To taste	Salt and black pepper

Method

Mix oil, honey, salt and lime juice then marinate the six snapper filets, let sit for 30–45 minutes.

Sauté red snapper filet in a large sauté pan with butter and oil.

Cook until done, 3–4 minutes on each side.

Remove from pan, add lemon juice and wine to pan, deglaze, and let cook until almost dissolved.

Add butter and whisk quickly.

Add parsley and season with salt and pepper.

Shrimp and Potato Hash

Ingredients

18 oz.	Small shrimp, peeled and deveined
3 oz. (as needed)	Olive oil
2 oz.	Butter
1 oz.	Bacon, chopped fine
2 oz.	Shallots, chopped fine

2 oz.	Fennel, chopped fine
2 oz.	Yellow onions, chopped fine
1 oz.	Garlic, chopped fine
6 oz.	Celery, diced small
18 oz.	Idaho Potatoes, cooked and diced small
4 oz.	Dry white wine
6 oz.	Fish or chicken stock
1 oz.	Chives, minced

Method

Heat a large sauté pan and add oil and butter.

Add bacon, shallots, fennel, onions, garlic, and celery; sauté for 3–5 minutes.

Add potatoes and brown lightly.

Cook for 2–3 minutes; add shrimp.

Continue cooking for 1–2 minutes or until shrimp is fully cooked.

Finish with wine, stock, salt, pepper, and chives.

Presentation

Place about 7–8 oz. of hash on a warm plate.

Place sautéed snapper filet on top and serve with pan sauce.

Shrimp and Pork Bolognese over Pasta
(8 servings)

Pork Sauce

Ingredients

1 oz.	Olive oil
4 oz.	Pancetta, diced
6 oz.	Onions, diced
4 oz.	Carrots, diced
4 oz.	Celery, diced
2 oz.	Olive oil
16 oz.	Boneless pork loin, finally diced
	Note: Try to purchase pork with some fat (not too lean) for a great flavor in the sauce.
2 tbsp.	Tomato paste
4 oz.	Red wine
8 oz.	Chicken broth
8 oz.	Diced tomatoes in juice
12 oz.	Tomato sauce
To taste	Kosher salt and crushed red pepper

Method

Heat 1 oz. olive oil in a pan.
Add pancetta, onion, carrots, and celery.
Cook until light brown.
Add 2 oz. olive oil to the pan.
Add pork and cook until browned.
Add tomato paste and mix well; cook 1–2 minutes longer.
Add wine and deglaze pan.
Add broth and cook for 1 minute.
Add tomatoes and sauce and simmer on low heat for 30 minutes.
Stir occasionally.
Season with kosher salt and crushed red pepper.

Shrimp

Ingredients

24 oz.	Shrimp (22/24 count), chopped
2 oz.	Extra virgin olive oil
1 oz.	Sage, chopped
3 oz.	Pesto
6 oz.	Heavy cream
2 oz.	Butter

Method

Sauté shrimp 2–3 minutes in 2 oz. olive oil.
Add sage and pesto, then cream.
Simmer 2–3 minutes, mixing well.

To Finish

Fold shrimp mixture into sauce with pork.
Simmer 10–15 minutes.
Serve over 1 lb. of your favorite pasta noodles or spaghetti.

Chef Mike's Lobster "Fra Diablo"
(4 servings)

Ingredients

4	Live lobsters, 1¼ lb. average
	Note: if desired, purchase 2 lbs. of cleaned and picked lobster meat.
4 fl. oz.	Olive oil
1 tbsp.	Garlic, minced
1 tsp.	Crushed red pepper (plus or minus depending on personal taste)
¼ tsp.	Fresh oregano lightly minced
2 tbsp.	Fresh basil leaf sliced in ⅛" strips
2 tbsp.	Fresh parsley, destemmed and minced
2 fl. oz.	Brandy
6 fl. oz.	Merlot
24 fl. oz.	Tomato sauce, homemade or your favorite brand
To taste	Salt and pepper
1 lb.	Fresh pasta—linguini, spaghetti, or capellini—cooked
	Chopped parsley for garnish

Method

Cut and split lobsters.

Heat up large skillet (preferably stainless steel or nonstick), add olive oil, and sauté lobster lightly, browning flesh side as well as sautéing shell side.

Add minced garlic, fresh herbs, and crushed red pepper and sauté for 1 minute or until garlic turns light golden color.

Flame with brandy and add merlot; reduce to half.

Add tomato sauce and simmer for 5–7 minutes or until meat is fully cooked.

Do not overcook.

Adjust seasoning with salt and pepper.

Serve over warm pasta tossed in extra virgin olive oil with salt, pepper, chopped parsley, and 1 tbsp. whole butter.

Enjoy!

Battered Soft Shell Crabs over Linguini
(8 servings)

Ingredients

Batter

6	Eggs
1/4 cup	Parsley, chopped
1/4 cup	Chives, snipped
1/4 cup	Fresh basil, chopped fine
3 tbsp.	Extra virgin olive oil
1/4 cup	Parmesan cheese, grated
1/2 cup	Heavy cream

Soft Shell Crabs

8	Jumbo soft shell crabs, cleaned
As needed	Canola oil (about 1 1/2 cups)
3 tbsp.	Butter

Sauce

1 tbsp.	Shallots, peeled and minced
4 fl. oz.	White wine
	Juice of 1 lemon
1 pinch	Crushed red pepper
1 tbsp.	Capers
1 tbsp.	Tomato paste
2 cups	Chicken broth
2 cups	Plum tomatoes, peeled, seeded, and diced
1 bunch	Broccolini, blanched
To taste	Salt and pepper
2 oz.	Butter
	Seasoned flour
	Note: To make seasoned flour, combine 2 cups flour, 1 tbsp. Kosher salt, 2 tbsp. Spice de Cosette seasoning, and 1 tsp. black pepper. Mix well.
1 lb.	Fresh linguini, cooked
	Chopped parsley for garnish

Method

In large bowl, combine eggs, parsley, chives, basil, olive oil, and parmesan cheese.

Whip in heavy cream and reserve in a cool place.

Clean crabs or purchase cleaned and picked crabmeat.

Dredge crabs in seasoned flour and dip into the butter.

Over medium heat in a nonstick pan, sauté in oil and butter on both sides until golden brown.

Transfer to a baking sheet and hold in a 300° oven for 10–12 minutes while preparing pasta and sauce.

In sauté pan that crabs were cooked in, drain off fat, then add shallots and sauté lightly until translucent.

Add white wine, lemon juice, capers, and crushed red pepper and reduce by one half.

Add tomato paste and cook for 1 minute.

Add chicken broth and reduce by one third.

Add plum tomatoes, broccolini, and butter; adjust seasonings.

Place crabs over cooked pasta and top with sauce.

Serve immediately.

Poached Seafood with Bowtie Pasta, Fresh Spinach, and Strawberry Poppy Seed Dressing
(4 servings)

Poached Seafood

Ingredients

8	Sea scallops
12	Shrimp, cleaned and peeled
12	Prince Edward Island mussels, washed and cleaned
1/2 cup	White wine
1 cup	Chicken or fish broth
1	Lemon, cut in half
2 tbsp.	Butter
2 sprigs each	Thyme and tarragon
2 cups	Baby spinach, cleaned and picked
2	Shallots, sliced very thin
1	Cucumber, cleaned and deseeded and sliced thin
8	Strawberries, sliced thin
8 oz.	Bow tie pasta
3 tbsp.	Butter, diced

Method

In a shallow pan, bring wine, broth, lemon, butter, and herbs to a boil, then place on low simmer.

Poach mussels, scallops, and shrimp until cooked; remove from pan and reserve.

Strain poaching liquid and simmer until it reduces by two thirds.

Start cooking pasta.

Place all ingredients in a large bowl and gently toss with 6 oz. of the dressing.

When pasta is cooked al dente, remove from stove, drain well, and toss with the reduced poaching liquid and 3 tablespoons of cold butter.

Immediately toss with all salad items.

Place 3 shrimp, three mussels, and one scallop on each plate of salad.

Spoon over the seafood the remaining dressing, then serve.

Strawberry Poppy Seed Dressing

Ingredients

6 oz.	Extra virgin olive oil
2 oz.	12-year-old balsamic vinegar
4 oz.	Strawberry purée
To taste	Black pepper
1 tbsp.	Fresh tarragon, minced
1 tbsp.	Poppy seed

Method

Combine ingredients and mix well.

Reader's Notes and Thoughts

The Long Way to the Hotel

My first exhibition trip to Germany was such a memorable experience: the chefs, the daily awesome displays of food at the exhibition halls, and the hot food kitchens. I was still working with the New York team after Chef Fritz Sonnenschmidt won his gold medal. There were three more days of competition, and I was there for the long haul.

Frankfurt was different from the United States in many ways. I remember going to the hotel elevator. A very pretty lady also got in. She said, "How are you today?" I said, "Good, and you?"

She then said, "I would be better if you would make love to me."

I looked around to see whether there was another person in the elevator. I said, "Excuse me? I thought you said something else."

"What, you do not find me attractive?" she asked.

I answered, "Very much so."

"So again I ask, do you want to make love to me?"

I was feeling very good about myself until she explained that there was a price involved, so I got off on the next floor and thought it would be much better to go to work with the team.

We changed into our chef clothes and went over the game plan for the day. Before we began our work, however, we decided to have a bite to eat in the restaurant downstairs. In Europe, most breakfasts are in a buffet setting and the selection is very good. All 10 of us walked in and sat down. We waited a bit since the restaurant was busy.

After 20 minutes, the manager came by and asked if we would please leave and change our clothes. It seems that many customers complained that the wait was long and no wonder with all the chefs sitting down and eating instead of working.

Our team liaison did not take kindly to this and said, "We are your customers as well, and you should be proud to have a group of chefs from the States sitting here." It was not a pleasant experience, so we decided to go back to our regular clothes and not cause trouble.

After breakfast, we worked from the early morning until early the following morning. It was around 5:00 A.M. the following day when we went to the hall to set up and look around. The team manager, a very nice man named Helmut, offered to give me a ride back to my hotel and thanked me for my help.

I was not sure of the way as I pointed him toward the hotel and said I remembered something about taking the Autobahn. We started driving and talked for a while. It was great driving on the Autobahn—cars just zipping by at a nice, fast speed that was legal. I was really tired, and when Helmut asked if he was going in the right direction I said, "Yes, I think so. There is the hotel on the other side." That is the last I remember; I fell sound asleep.

I was awakened by a loud discussion. We were at a rest area, and Helmut was speaking German, waving his arms and pointing at me. He got back in the car and I asked what was wrong. What was wrong, he said, was that the hotel I pointed to from the highway was not my hotel. It was not in the center of Frankfurt, and we were about one hour away from my hotel, which was located 10 minutes from the exhibit hall.

He was not happy, since he was tired as well. He still had to pick up chefs from the hall, and we still had a good ride ahead of us, even at the Autobahn speed. I apologized and tried to have a cheery conversation, but he was not in a talking mood. I agree it was a long way to the hotel going my way, but what was one to do; I was just an apprentice and did not know!

Tomato, Basil, and Olive Tarts
(5 dozen small tarts)

Ingredients

4 oz.	Parmesan cheese, grated
4 oz.	Fresh mozzarella, grated
8	Tomatoes, seeded and chopped
1/2 cup	Basil, thinly sliced
1/2 cup	Olives, pitted and chopped
	Note: You can use Kalamata olives for a sharp flavor or plain black olives.
To taste	Kosher salt
2 tbsp.	Extra virgin olive oil
6 large	Eggs
2 tbsp.	Virgin olive oil
6 oz.	Half & half
To taste	Salt and Pepper
5 doz.	Small tart shells

Method

Mix first 7 ingredients together let sit for 30 minutes.
Mix eggs, 2 tbsp. olive oil, half & half, salt, and pepper well.
Fill each shell with 1 part tomato and cheese mixture and then two parts egg mixture.
Bake for 20–30 minutes until filling is set.

Cheddar Cheese Soup
(6 servings)

Ingredients

4 oz.	Butter
4 oz.	Flour
2 pts.	Chicken stock, hot
3 oz.	Celery, diced ½"
3 oz.	Carrots, diced ½"
2 oz.	Onion, chopped
12 oz.	Sharp cheddar cheese, grated
½ tsp.	Paprika
½ oz.	Cornstarch
½ oz.	Sugar
To taste	Salt
6 oz.	Ale
4 oz.	Cream, hot
¾ oz.	Worcestershire sauce
2 oz.	Butter, diced

Method

Melt butter, add flour, and blend well.
Add hot stock and mix well.
Let simmer for 3–5 minutes.
Add vegetables and simmer slowly for ½ hour or until vegetables are tender.
Over low heat, whisk in cheese; continue to simmer until cheese melts.
Combine dry ingredients; add ale to make a smooth paste.
Stir into soup and simmer 10 minutes longer; remove from heat.
Add hot cream, butter, and Worcestershire sauce.
Adjust seasoning and serve with croutons.

BLT Soup with Rye Croutons
(12 servings)

Ingredients

3/4 cup	Bacon grease
2	Sweet onions, chopped
1 clove	Garlic, minced
1/2 oz.	Custom Gold mirepoix base
3 oz.	Sweet butter
3 heads	Romaine lettuce, finely shredded
1 cup	Flour
1 1/4 qts.	Chicken broth
To taste	Salt or high-quality chicken base
1 1/2 pts.	Light cream, heated
1 cup	Milk
5	Plum tomatoes, diced
1 1/2 lbs.	Cooked bacon, chopped
To taste	Salt and pepper
6 slices	Hearty rye bread, cubed
7 tbsp.	High-quality mayonnaise
2 tbsp.	Fresh sage
1 oz.	Sweet butter

Method

Heat 1/4 cup grease in soup pan.
Sauté onion and garlic.
Add mirepoix base, butter, and remaining bacon grease.
Add romaine and sauté 2–3 minutes.
Reserve 6 oz. of romaine.
Add flour and cook until light brown.
Add broth and chicken base; bring to a simmer.
Add cream, milk, one half of tomatoes, and one half of bacon.
Simmer until proper consistency.
Add remainder of tomatoes and bacon. Season.
Toast bread cubes in oven; reserve.
Mix mayonnaise with remaining romaine, bacon, tomato, and sage.
Garnish soup bowls with mayonnaise mixture and croutons.
Finish soup with butter and pour into bowls.

Braised Pork Rolls and Sausage
(5 servings)

Pork Rolls

Ingredients

1/4 cup	Pine nuts (pignoli), toasted golden
1/2 cup	Italian parsley, chopped fine, leaves only
3 cups	Bread, dried, crust removed, cut in 1" cubes
1 1/2 cups	Milk
2 tbsp.	Garlic, minced
1/4 cup	Parmigiano reggiano, finely grated
1/4 cup	Pecorino
1/2 cup	Raisins, soft, golden or brown
1/4 lb.	Prosciutto, sliced thin
10 slices	Provolone, cut thin
To taste	Salt and black pepper
10 pieces	Pork cutlets cut from the pork butt and pounded thin

Method

Soak bread in milk until soft; squeeze out milk.
Mix bread with pine nuts, raisins, parsley, parmigiano, pecorino, and garlic; season with salt and pepper.
Cover each slice of pork with a small piece of prosciutto.
Spread filling over end of slices, leaving about 1/2-inch edge.
Lay a slice of provolone over the filling.
Roll up, folding the edges over, and tie into bundles with string.

Sauce

Ingredients

As needed	Extra virgin olive oil
12 cloves	Garlic, peeled and crushed
1 cup	Red wine
2 qts.	Italian tomatoes, peeled
1	Bay leaf
To taste	Salt and red pepper flakes
1 lb.	Fennel sausage

Method

Heat enough oil to lightly cover the bottom of a pan.
Season pork rolls with salt and pepper.
Brown in oil until golden; drain and reserve.
Add garlic cloves and gently cook until golden brown. Remove and discard.
Deglaze pan with red wine and reduce until almost dry.
Add tomatoes passed through the medium blade of a food mill (with liquid), and bring to a simmer.
Note: You may use strained tomatoes if you prefer.
Season with salt and pepper, add red pepper flakes, and add pork rolls.
Bring to simmer and cook until just barely fork tender.
Heat enough olive oil to film a pan.
Add sausage and brown slowly over low heat until brown.
Add to sauce about 30 minutes before pork is done.
Let sauce and meat rest 30 minutes, skim off fat.
Remove string and serve with 1 lb. of your favorite pasta tossed with sauce.
Serve with a mixture of parmigiano and pecorino cheese and chopped basil and parsley.

Spiced Shrimp and Yucca Over Rice
(8–10 servings)

Ingredients

2 lbs.	Shrimp, cleaned and peeled
2 lbs.	Yucca root, peeled and diced, soaked in cold water 1 hour
1 pt.	Shrimp stock
	Juice of 1 lime
To taste	Salt and pepper
1 large	Onion, quartered
3	Whole cloves
1	Bay leaf
4 tbsp.	Extra virgin olive oil
2 medium	Onions, diced
2	Garlic cloves, sliced
10	Plum tomatoes, peeled and seeded
1 tbsp.	Tomato paste
1 cup	Light cream
1 cup	Coconut milk
2 tbsp.	Chili oil
4 tbsp.	Heavy cream
1/2 cup	Cilantro, chopped
1/2 cup	Parsley, chopped
4–5 cups	White rice, cooked

Method

Mix shrimp with lime juice and some salt and pepper.

Drain the yucca and place in a large pot of salted water.

Stud one onion quarter with cloves; add it and the remaining quarters and bay leaf to the pot.

Cook until fork tender.

Drain yucca and onions and cool slightly. Remove the bay leaf, cloves, and any fibrous cords from the yucca.

Reserve the yucca and onion quarters.

In a large, heavy skillet, heat oil and cook the diced onions and garlic until light brown.
Add shrimp and cook on both sides until bright pink and tender.
Remove shrimp, add tomatoes and tomato paste, then deglaze with stock.
Season and keep stirring while simmering for 10–12 minutes.
In a food processor or blender, puree yucca, onions, tomato mixture, cream, coconut milk, and oil.
Place in a saucepan, add herbs and heavy cream, season, and cook for 5–7 minutes.
Adjust consistency with more stock or cream.
Add shrimp for 1 minute more.
Serve over rice, 1/2 cup per person.

The Dutch and Their Shoes

*I*n the world of culinary competition, two things are special and a true benefit of competing. One is the education and the chance to improve your skills. The second is the people you meet along the way who may influence your life and become great friends.

Every four years the largest cookery show in the world is held in Germany. It brings more than 28 countries together in a week of cookery and fraternal friendship.

Many chefs from all over the world show their cuisine to a panel of international judges who award medals based on the quality of work.

Even though chefs can enter on their own, only one recognized team from each country is allowed to compete and represent their country in the hot kitchen as well as the cold buffet. I had read about this competition during my apprenticeship and had a copy of the 1976 Culinary Olympics book featuring the 1976 team of chefs from the American Culinary Federation.

Many of the judges who had rated my infamous sushi platter were present or past members of the culinary team. A judge who always gave me the hardest critiques was Chef Fritz Sonnenschmidt. He was a Certified Master Chef (CMC), a member of the 1976 and 1980 USA American Culinary Federation National teams, and a head instructor at the Culinary Institute of America in 1983. (Unknown to me at the time, Chef Fritz would become a mentor and my dear friend of 20-plus years as I trained to become a chef.)

In 1984 I received a call and was asked by a chef friend if I wanted to go to that year's Culinary Olympics in Germany. We would travel there and work for the New York Regional team. We would be assigned a chef to work with and have a once-in-a-lifetime experience.

I was so excited. I jumped on this opportunity and could not wait, but there was one catch: We had to pay our airfare and hotel bill (they would cover meals and the show pass). Still, it did not matter. I was on my first trip to Europe and my first time at the largest international show. I wanted to be a team member at this exhibition one day. The thrill of being in a new country and having the chance to cook with some great chefs—what more could I want?

When we arrived, we took one day to rest and adjust to the time change, which in itself was very interesting (see my "Into the Sauna" story). The next day we arrived at the Frankfurt Sheraton and met the team. I was assigned to work with the chef I feared the most, Fritz Sonnenschmidt, CMC.

A couple of days went by. I did whatever Chef needed, and he took me with him to a traditional German restaurant to eat during our breaks. We talked of food, and he educated me on his life experiences. The passion he had when he spoke of food and cooking was just amazing, and for a young aspiring chef it was a great feeling to be with such a master of cookery.

On the final night before Chef was to display, we were working feverishly to get things done. He came to me and said, "I have a very important job for you if you are up to it."

Well, I was not going to let Chef down, so I said, "Yes, I am. Just show me what you want."

He took me to a counter on which many pears, a cutting board, and a few small paring knifes sat. With much grace and speed he carved a pear half into a Dutch shoe or clog. He was going to marinate these shoes and fill them with a grape garnish.

I stood there and hesitantly asked him to show me once more. He was a master, and when it came to garde (the craft of the cold kitchen chef), one of the best. To him carving was second nature. He did one more and said, "Now, do 24 perfect shoes for me, then toss them in the marinade and place them on a tray." It was midnight at this point, and Chef had to be at the exhibit hall by 7:00 A.M. to display his food.

Chef disappeared, and I stood there trying to carve 24 perfect Dutch shoes for him. Needless to say, it took me many pears to get the hang of this and then carve 24 perfect ones. Shortly after 3:00 A.M. I had finished the shoes. Twenty-four perfect Dutch shoes made out of pears, marinated and ready for display.

Chef appeared looking all refreshed. He had a new chef's coat and was shaven. "It must be nice to shower and get rest," I thought, but this was the price of apprenticeship. He looked at the pear shoes while holding an empty tray. I asked nervously, "What is wrong, Chef?"

Did I mess up? Were they not good enough? He said, "Just looking for the best." The best, I wondered. He said 24. Did I need to make more? Were some not that good?

He placed one in his mouth and ate it, then he ate another one. Apprentice or not, this was going too far! He then placed nine of the shoes on the tray, ate another one, and said, "Thanks. I have what I need. Please clean up."

I was not happy and stammered, "What about the other ones? You said 24."

He just looked at me and said, "Young Leonard, I needed 9 really perfect ones, so I figured if you carved 24 I would at least get that," and he walked away. My face was red, and I wanted to throw the rest of the shoes at him as he disappeared into the cooler.

When we went to the hall, I did not speak to Chef. We set up his food display, and I looked at all the other culinary marvels on display from all over the world in pure amazement.

Well, Chef Fritz received a gold medal for his work and went out of his way to thank me as we both enjoyed a great dinner of pork shank, potatoes, and more.

In the years to come I would realize that the Dutch shoes and many other lessons were designed to push me and make me the best I could be. I would also realize that Chef Fritz was a great culinarian, but most of all he was a humble person who was full of life and passion and set the standard for giving back to those who want to learn.

As my career went forward, I was to fulfill my dream of competing at the Culinary Olympics and getting my first international gold medal. I even exceeded my dreams by becoming the captain of the 2000 and 2004 ACF Culinary Team USA. Much is owed to my mentor and Dutch shoe friend, Chef Fritz.

Roast Lamb Shanks with Lentils
(4 servings)

Ingredients

2 cloves	Garlic, sliced paper thin
4	Lamb shanks (1 lb. each)
To taste	Salt
To taste	Black pepper
3 tbsp.	Vegetable oil
2 tbsp.	Butter
1/2 cup	Onion, finely chopped
2 1/2 cups	Beef stock
2 1/2 cups	Lentils, thoroughly washed and drained
1	Bay leaf
1/2 cup	Scallions, chopped
1/4 cup	Fresh parsley, chopped

Method

Using a knife, insert 3 garlic slivers into the meaty portion of the lamb shanks.

Sprinkle shanks generously with salt and a few grindings of pepper.

Heat oil in a pan over high heat; add shanks and cook over moderate heat until all sides are browned.

Transfer shanks to a rack in a shallow roasting pan, and roast for 1 hour in 350° oven.

Melt two tbsp. butter and cook onions until transparent but not brown.

Pour in the stock, add lentils, bay leaf, salt, and black pepper, bring to a boil, cover, then simmer until all stock is absorbed (30 minutes).

Café Choucroute
(Sauerkraut)
(6 servings)

Ingredients

3 lbs.	Sauerkraut, rinsed well
4 oz	Bacon or duck fat
4 tbsp.	Sugar
2 oz	Duck fat
2	Onions, diced
2 cups	Riesling wine
1 cup	Chicken stock
6	Pork chops, 1 inch thick, cut from the back end, seasoned with salt and freshly ground black pepper to taste
2	Whole cloves
6	Juniper berries
2	Bay leaves
4 cloves	Garlic
6	Bratwurst
6	High-quality frankfurters
1 lb.	Garlic sausage
1 lb.	Smoked pork sausage
2 lbs.	New potatoes
1 lb.	Smoked slab bacon, cut into large pieces

Method

Preheat the oven to 350°.

Sauté the sauerkraut with the fat and sugar for 3–4 minutes; reserve.

Grill pork chops for 2–3 minutes on each side over high heat.

In a large casserole over low heat, melt the fat, add the onions, and sauté until soft.

Add the wine and broth.

Add the pork chops, cover with the sauerkraut, and add the pepper, cloves, juniper berries, bay leaves, and garlic. Cover and bake for 15 minutes.

In a cast iron or other heavy pan, sear all the sausages; add to casserole and cook 20 minutes more.

Boil the potatoes. Allow them to cool just enough to handle, and then peel. Toss with some butter or olive oil and keep warm.

Grill the slab bacon pieces until very crisp.

On a large platter, place potatoes and bacon, then the sausages, chops, and sauerkraut.

Serve with spicy mustard and bread.

Braised Oxtails
(6–8 servings)

Ingredients

6 lbs.	Oxtails, cut into 4-inch-thick pieces
4 tbsp.	Flour
4 tbsp.	Olive oil
3 cups	Onion, coarsely chopped
4	Carrots, coarsely chopped
3 stalks	Celery, coarsely chopped
3 large cloves	Garlic, finely minced
6 sprigs	Fresh thyme
4	Bay leaves
1 cup	Red wine
2 cups	Beef broth
2 tbsp.	Tomato paste
To taste	Sea salt
To taste	Freshly ground black pepper

Method

Preheat oven to 425°.
Roast oxtails on a rack for 15–20 minutes to remove excess fat. Remove and let cool.
Season each piece with sea salt and pepper, then dust with flour.
Heat olive oil in an 8-quart heavy-bottomed casserole pan over medium heat.
Brown the oxtail pieces in batches until all sides are dark brown.
Remove each batch to a platter. Do not let the pan drippings get too brown.
After all of the oxtail pieces have been browned, pour off excess fat and add the onion, carrots, celery, garlic, and bay leaves.
Place the pot back on the stove over medium heat and cook stirring occasionally for 10–15 minutes. Vegetables should be lightly browned.
Stir in the tomato paste and cook 3–4 minutes then add red wine, stock, and thyme sprigs; stir to combine. Add the browned oxtail pieces with their juices, cover and place in a 325° oven for at least 2 hours until fork tender.
Remove the casserole from the oven.

With a spoon, remove the braised oxtails to a heated platter. Discard bay leaves and thyme sprigs. Place the liquid in a saucepan and bring to high heat, then simmer on low heat until reduced.

Skim any fat that rises to the surface.

Season the sauce with salt and pepper.

Return the oxtails to the pan and heat through.

Serve over polenta or roasted garlic, mashed.

Roast Pork with Balsamic Apples and Onions
(8 servings)

Ingredients

1	Pork loin roast, cut toward the butt end and tied
2 tsp.	Kosher salt
1 tsp.	Crushed red pepper
3 tbsp.	Olive oil
2 tbsp.	Butter
4	Sweet onions, peeled and cut in half and sliced thin
2 cloves	Garlic, peeled and cut in half
1/2 cup	Unsalted butter
2 tbsp.	Chiffonade of basil
1 1/2 cups	12-year-old balsamic vinegar
2 tbsp.	Honey
1/4 cup	Red wine
3 tbsp.	Flat leaf parsley, minced
3 tbsp.	Cold butter, diced

Method

Season the meat with the salt and pepper, rubbing it into the entire surface of the roast. Set aside.

Heat a large cast iron skillet over high heat, add the olive oil, and add the roast.

Reduce temperature to medium-high heat and continue to sear until deep golden brown on all sides.

Remove the roast to a platter.

Heat a large roasting pan over medium heat on top of the stove. Add olive oil and butter.

When the butter has melted, add the onions, garlic and apples and cook until translucent, about 10 minutes.

Add the basil and stir to combine.

Add 3/4 cup vinegar and broth.

Place the seared pork loin roast on top of the onions and baste with the vinegar and apple and onion juices. Place the roast into a preheated 350° oven and roast.

After 15 minutes of cooking, turn the roast and baste with the mixture, stirring.

Continue to cook for an additional 30–40 minutes, until a meat thermometer reads 140°. Add remaining ¾ cup balsamic vinegar to the roasting pan 10 minutes before the roast is to be removed from the oven. Remove the roast to a cake rack over a carving board and allow it to rest for 15 minutes before carving.

Place the roasting pan on top of the stove and deglaze the onions and meat drippings with the red wine. Bring to a boil over high heat and simmer until the mixture has reduced again to a thick consistency. Mix in butter and season.

Slice the roast and serve with large spoonfuls of the balsamic apples and onions.

Serve with mashed potatoes and your favorite vegetable.

Note: At the Westchester Country Club, we purchase Niman Ranch pork for our pork recipes and highly recommend it.

Reader's Notes and Thoughts

Into the Sauna

*B*eing a chef is very hard work. The long hours are both physically and mentally demanding. We do, however, have time to play and relax on occasion. At certain times in your career, you play as hard as you work. I would have to put most of my tales of those occasions in another book, and I'm not sure I could publish it for a general audience.

My first visit to Frankfurt for the culinary competition was wonderful. I checked into the Ramada Carousel, a quaint German hotel with many amenities and two nice restaurants. I washed up and went to have breakfast. What a buffet! The food was very different from what we have—many platters of meats, sausages, salamis, and cheeses graced the breakfast table.

After breakfast, I went for a walk and looked at the markets. The food markets are really special in Europe, offering a huge variety of in-season products of the finest quality. There was also an upstairs floor where fresh-cut meats, suckling pig, and the best bratwurst I ever tasted were sold.

Later I took another walk with a chef friend who was traveling with me. We kept walking and somehow got lost trying to get back to the hotel. Our German was not very good, and we stopped a couple of times to ask directions but could not find an English-speaking person. In fact, asking for directions in German made it worse because the person would answer back in fluent German. We approached one man who looked at us closely, listened carefully, and then said, "No speak English." This was hopeless. I walked away, saying, "We really need to get back and get some rest so we can get to the kitchens at the Sheraton Hotel."

After we had walked a few feet, the man yelled out, so we turned around. He said, "By the way, go two blocks and take a right, go another three blocks and take a left, and you will be on your way to the hotel. You should have told me you were chefs." He let out a burly laugh and left. We laughed as well and made our way to the hotel for some rest so we could adjust to the time change before working with the culinary team.

I went to my room, but I was wide awake, so I read a bit and then looked through the hotel book of services. I saw that there was a nice pool and sauna in the hotel.

I thought, "Wow, a sauna, a steam room, a nice swim, and I'll be able to get a great sleep after that!" I took a shower, found my bathing suit, got dressed, and headed to the pool and sauna area. I went into the locker room to change and lock up my clothes and then headed to the sauna in my swim trunks, with a towel around my neck. Ah, this was going to be great. I could not wait to lie down and have the hot steam relax me. I went toward the door and noticed a row of open showers with no curtains. Odd, they must be cleaning them.

There was also a nice-sized balcony with both doors wide open, so I went and shut the doors and headed to the sauna. I opened the sauna door, stepped in, removed the towel, and looked up. My mouth dropped open and I froze. Two totally naked ladies were there in front of me. One was sitting with the towel off to her side, and the other was just lying there with her legs up in the air, speaking to the first woman. They looked at me and said hello in German. I, on the other hand, said, "Sorry, very sorry. Have a great day." And I ran from the sauna.

At first I hoped they would not call security, then I looked for the men's sauna. I could not find it, so I just sat back and stared toward the sauna room. The two women emerged, still naked. They showered and went out on the balcony for about three minutes. Then they both put on towels and walked toward the ladies locker room, giving me a wink and a wave. I was to find out later that the sauna was for men and women. The showers were unisex, and the balcony was used to air out after a sauna and a shower. In Germany, this was not a big deal.

Since that time, I have shared bathrooms with ladies in Italy and Spain and have taken showers where men and women showered in stalls with no dividers or curtains. I have even had to use an old toilet that you squat over, since there were no Western-style toilets available.

Yes, my journey was teaching me many things in life besides cookery. When in Rome do as the Romans do!

Sweet Potato Pie
(8 servings)

Ingredients

³/₄ cup	Sugar
1 tbsp.	All-purpose flour, sifted
¹/₂ tsp.	Baking powder
¹/₄ tsp.	Salt
1 tsp.	Cinnamon
¹/₂ tsp.	Nutmeg, fresh grated
¹/₄ tsp.	Allspice
2 cups	Sweet potatoes, hot, cooked and mashed
³/₄ cup	Sweet butter, diced
1 tbsp.	Fresh lime juice
1 tsp.	Real vanilla extract
1 tsp.	Maple syrup
1 large	Egg
1 cup	Half & half

Method

Combine first seven items and mix with a whisk.
Place potatoes in a bowl and gently mix in butter.
Blend in dry items; mix until smooth.
Add lime juice, vanilla, and maple syrup.
Mix eggs with cream, then fold into potato mixture.
Pour filling into shell, cover edges, and bake at 425° for 12–15 minutes.
Finish baking at 375° for 40–45 minutes until top is set and crust is golden brown.

Maple Pecan Pie
(8 servings)

Ingredients

4 tbsp.	Sweet butter
¾ cup	Granulated Sugar
¼ tsp.	Salt
4 large	Eggs
1 cup	Grade A pure maple syrup
6 oz.	Pecans
1	8-inch pie crust

Method

Slowly toast pecans. Cool, then chop. Do not burn.
Melt butter; mix in sugar and salt.
Beat in eggs, then syrup.
Place on double boiler and stir until shiny and warm (130°).
Stir in pecans.
Pour into pie crust and bake 45–60 minutes until filling is set.
Let cool for at least 5 hours on a cake rack in a cool place.

Frozen Banana Parfait with Banana Sauce
(8 servings)

Parfait

Ingredients

2 lbs.	Bananas, peeled
1 tsp.	Fresh lemon juice
2 tbsp.	Myers dark rum
12 oz.	Heavy cream
4 oz.	Sugar
1 tsp.	Real vanilla extract
2 oz.	Roasted peanuts, chopped

Method

Puree bananas, strain, place in bowl, and stir in lemon juice.
Mix cream, sugar, and vanilla until soft peaks form; fold into purée.
Pipe into molds, sprinkle with peanuts, and freeze.

Sauce

Ingredients

1¹/₂ qts.	Heavy cream
1 lb.	Bananas, split lengthwise
12 oz.	Granulated sugar

Method

Place cream and bananas in saucepot and bring to boil.
Cover, remove from heat, and let steep for 20 minutes.
Strain and set aside.
Caramelize sugar over high heat until amber.
Stir in heavy cream mixture and bring to a boil, strain and cool.

Vanilla Sauce
(3 pints)

Ingredients

1 pt.	Milk
1 pt.	Heavy cream
1	Vanilla bean
8 oz.	Sugar
9 oz.	Egg yolks

Method

Heat milk, heavy cream, vanilla bean, and half of the sugar until it boils.
Remove the vanilla bean and reserve for other uses.
Combine egg yolks and the remaining sugar, then temper with part of the boiling milk while stirring constantly.
Pour liaison (egg yolk mixture) into the remaining milk and return to heat.
Stirring constantly, cook slowly to stage of nappe (i.e., coats the back of a spoon), or 180°.
Remove immediately from stove and strain through a chinois directly into a bain marie in an ice bath.

Chocolate Sauce
(2 cups)

Ingredients

1 pt.	Heavy cream
2 oz.	Honey
2 oz.	Corn syrup
To taste	Vanilla extract
16 oz.	Chocolate, melted
3 oz.	Butter, diced
1 oz.	Cocoa butter (optional)

Method

In a stainless steel saucepan, combine heavy cream, honey, and corn syrup.
Bring to a boil and remove from heat.
Add vanilla and chocolate and mix well.
Fold in butter and cocoa butter if desired.
Let cool.

Caramel Sauce
(2–3 cups)

Ingredients

4 oz.	Sugar
2 fluid oz.	Water
$\frac{1}{2}$ qt.	Milk or heavy cream
2 oz.	Egg yolks

Method

Note: Use only a stainless steel pan.

Melt sugar until it is a caramel color.
Add the water; stir until smooth and caramel sugar is melted.
Add milk and eggs; cook until the sauce coats the back of a spoon.
Serve warm.

Reader's Notes and Thoughts

One of a Kind

I remember my first trip to London, England. I was going to compete in the Hotel Olympia competition, which was held every two years. It was a great tour through England; I got to see many things, eat some great food, and learn quite a bit. I was assigned a chef who acted as my guide and helped me with the Olympia competition.

This was my first international competition, and I was excited and ready to see how I would do in another country. I worked at a hotel called Grosvenor House in the center of London, where I had done some training. It was a great experience to see all these chefs get ready for the day's meals and some who were entering the Hotel Olympia competition.

I worked very hard on my platter. It was to be something special that would be sure to wow the judges. I even had help from chefs at the CIA, such as Chef Fritz, who had coached me in a few of the intricate things I had in mind. My platter was to feature a pork pâté with a braided dough of pumpernickel and rye, two more pork-type pieces, garnishes, and, for the final piece that would wow everyone, an apple mousse poured and layered into a mold that would resemble an apple right down to the skin.

I started the long process of making my mold and getting all other items ready for the mousse. My dough for the pâté was ready, and I was just starting on the garnishes. Other chefs came by and wished me well. They looked at my stuff with a few inquiries about the mousse and remarked on how forward-thinking my display looked. This should have set off an alarm, but it did not. I took it as a compliment.

I worked feverishly through the evening in the corner space that I was given. The sous-chefs invited me to dine with them, and we spoke of food, cultures, and the reputation of the United States as being a hamburger and hot dog kind of country. I did not get into a big debate on this because I was outnumbered. Not being an accomplished chef yet, I felt that discussing this with chefs from a country famous for fish and chips, roast beef, and a dish called "bangers and mashed" would be a futile effort.

I went back to work, got a bit of rest, and then set up my platter for the exhibit. The chef I was with took me to the hall. We registered and were given a number for our space. The entrance to the hall was huge, and inside the hall were table upon table of food displays, pastry displays, and some breathtaking work.

I went over to the table for pork and meat buffet platters and walked carefully so I wouldn't drop or move anything on my display. As I got to the table with the chef and saw the other 30-odd entries, my mouth dropped open and I shook my head.

The chef said, "What is wrong, mate? You have some bloody good work there." But mine was nothing close to the other platters of work. Mine was so, so different. Contemporary perhaps? Yes, it certainly was one of kind.

The chef explained that the exhibition was based on classical work from many years ago and that the English chefs and organizers were very traditional and were proud of that fact. "Well," I said, "this is not good for me, is it?"

He said. "I do not know, but every time things change and go forward, some person needs to be the one to bring it forward."

I set the silver platter down with my work, which stood out like a lighted Christmas tree in a dark room. It did have nice, clean lines; the apple turned out just perfectly, and it really did have style.

I looked at the rest of the show and took many pictures of some great work. The chef was correct. It was all classically based, featuring truffle paintings, decorated hams, and turkeys covered in a white sauce called *chaud fraud* and then decorated. Then there was the potato exhibit, which was incredible. The potatoes were carved into the shapes of boats, houses, and other buildings and were then fried. It was truly something to see.

Next, I toured the hot kitchen cookery competitions and saw some great cooks preparing food in a timed situation under the watchful eyes of the judges.

The day was almost over, and the awards were being placed on all of the cold food displays. After waiting a bit, I went toward the meat buffet table and saw many ribbons of gold, silver, bronze, and merit. I did not see anything near my platter at all, not even a ribbon of merit for much hard work and some nice items.

The chef saw my disappointment and tried to cheer me up. He said, "Look, you still have the fish category in two days. We will get them then."

One of the judges came over. He shook my hand, introduced himself to me, greeted Chef, whom he already knew, and looked at me. "America, I guess," he said simply.

I replied, "Yes, that's where I am from." You could tell this platter was one of a kind for the exhibit. He went on to lecture me about my platter and my mousse and even said, "You probably learned this from Chef Fritz and others from the United States team. We do not do this here; we cook very classically to show our craft. This direction will never catch on here. I hope you will learn because your skills are very good, but your training needs to be different."

I left the hall with mixed emotions and even some anger.

During next two days I went to work planning my fish platter. I would have a more practical approach to this but still keep a bit of my style.

It paid off. Although my platter was still one of kind in the fish category, it did have some of the traits the others had in style and technique. It garnered a bronze medal.

This was my first international medal, and I was proud. The whole experience in England, which would be my first of many trips, taught me so much. First, know the playing field and adapt to it, because it will not adapt to you. Second, learn a country's culture and food before making assumptions based on perception. I also learned that a style or method that does not work the first time may work in the future with some adjustments and patience.

The United States has become a very good representative of fine food in the international arena. Our European colleagues respect the food we cook and prepare. The team of chefs from the American Culinary Federation is a team that all countries can learn from and consider a threat in worldwide competitions. In 2003, the team tied with Canada for third in the world based on medal scores and placement in approved competitions since 1999. I am proud that I have been part of that team of chefs since 1999, and I am currently the team captain. It brings such a sense of pride to show what we can do. The food we were making back in those classical days now sets the tone for all international shows.

In the years that came after my exhibition in England, I would work for an English company called TrustHouse Forte for 13 years and learn that England has great food, great restaurants, and great chefs. When visiting outside of the United States, I urge all readers to learn about the country before you travel and adapt to its culture. It will show people from other countries that you have respect for them and have taken the time to learn about them prior to your visit. This goes a long way in making friends and gaining respect.

I often see Americans wanting to make foreign food more American when they travel. You are a visitor. If you want the comforts of home, do not travel, because you will not be happy. Embrace the changes. Learn, have fun, and enjoy the unique surroundings and the fine cuisine you will eat when abroad.

Life can be an exciting experience, and the journey can be a great one with lasting memories that are one of a kind.

Pinot Grigio Sauce
(2 cups)

Ingredients

4 oz.	Butter
2 tbsp.	Olive oil
1/4 cup each	Small dice of onion, celery, carrots, and leek
2 cloves	Garlic, sliced very thin
2 tsp.	Tomato paste
1 cup	Pinot Grigio
1 1/2 cups	Chicken broth
1 cup	Lobster broth (If sauce is not used for seafood then go with all chicken broth)
2 sprigs	Oregano, chopped
1/2 cup	Dried porcini pieces, soaked in 1 cup heavy cream
3 tbsp.	Ice cold butter, diced

Roux

2 tbsp.	Butter
2 tbsp.	Flour

Method

In a 2-qt. saucepan, sauté vegetables in butter and oil for 3–4 minutes.

Add garlic and sauté for another 2–3 minutes.

Add tomato paste and cook 1–2 minutes.

Deglaze the pan with Pinot Grigio; simmer until reduced in half.

Add chicken broth and lobster broth, bring to a boil, and simmer for 10 minutes.

Melt the butter for the roux in a small saucepan. Stir in flour and cook while stirring for 2–3 minutes.

Pour 8 oz. of the hot broth into the roux and whisk well.

Into the pot of broth and vegetables, whisk in the roux and broth and mix well.

Add oregano, bring to a simmer, and let cook 3–5 minutes.

Add cream and porcinis; simmer another 5 minutes.

Finish with cold butter, adjust seasoning, and serve over your favorite pasta with seafood or chicken dish.

Pan-Seared Pancetta-Wrapped Cod
(4 servings)

Ingredients

8 oz.	Fresh codfish
12 slices	Pancetta, sliced thin
6 leaves	Fresh sage, chopped fine
To taste	Black pepper

Method

Cut cod into four 2-oz. pieces.
Season cod with black pepper and fresh sage.
Place three slices of pancetta flat on a cutting board. Wrap pancetta evenly around one piece of cod.
Repeat for all pieces of fish. Refrigerate until ready for use.
When ready to serve, heat 2 oz. of blended oil in a nonstick sauté pan.
Brown fish evenly on all sides.
Roast in a 400° oven until fish is thoroughly cooked.

Chef Moose's Award-Winning Clam Sauce
(2 cups)

Ingredients

2 slices	Smoked bacon, chopped small
2 oz.	Onion, diced small
2 oz.	Celery, diced small
1 clove	Garlic, sliced thin
6 oz.	Butter, diced small
2 oz.	All-purpose flour
12 oz.	Clam broth
1 cup	Idaho potatoes, diced small
1/2 oz.	Tabasco sauce
8 oz.	Fresh or frozen clam meat, chopped
2 ears	Sweet corn, roasted and shucked
8 oz.	Heavy cream
2 tbsp.	Fresh thyme, finely chopped
1 oz.	Anise honey
1	Plum tomato, peeled, seeded, diced small
2 tbsp.	Butter, diced

Method

In a 2-qt. saucepan, render bacon.

Add butter, garlic, celery, and onions. Cook until tender.

Add flour and continue to cook for 2 minutes while stirring constantly.

After the 2 minutes, add the clam broth and stir until smooth. Add potatoes.

Bring to a light simmer and continue to cook, stirring occasionally, until the sauce has a nice consistency.

Add Tabasco and clam meat and simmer for 3–5 minutes.

Mix cream and corn with the clam broth; simmer for 2–3 minutes.

Add tomatoes and butter and season with salt and pepper.

Serve over pasta or pieces of roasted cod, halibut, or scrod.

Clam Fritters
(12 fritters)

Ingredients

1 cup	All-purpose flour
1/2 tsp.	Baking powder
1/4 tsp.	Kosher salt
1/8 cup	Sugar
1	Egg
1/2 cup	Stout beer
2 oz.	Extra virgin olive oil
1 tsp.	Fresh thyme, chopped fine
1 tsp.	Fresh sage, chopped fine
3 oz.	Florida hard shell clam meat, chopped
3 cups	Duck fat

Method

Into a medium mixing bowl, sift together the flour, baking powder, salt, and sugar.

Whisk in the egg and extra virgin olive oil until incorporated.

Add beer and herbs, and whisk until smooth.

Fold in the clam meat; cover mixture with plastic and reserve.

At time of serving, heat 3 cups of duck fat to 350° in a 2-qt. saucepan.

Using a teaspoon, drop 12 individual fritters into hot fat.

Cook through until golden brown.

Remove from fat and place onto paper towel to drain.

Sautéed Asparagus
(4 servings)

Ingredients

20 stalks	Fresh asparagus (pencil)
3 cups	Chicken broth
1 tsp.	Shallots, minced
1 tbsp.	Olive oil
4 oz.	Cold butter, diced
1 tsp.	Kosher salt

Method

In a 2-qt. saucepan, bring chicken broth to a rapid boil; add salt.
Drop asparagus into broth and cook until tender (approximately 1–2 minutes).
Remove from saucepan and place directly into refrigerator.
Reduce stock to half; reserve.
At time of serving, heat oil in a medium sauté pan over medium heat.
Add shallots and cook for 2 minutes.
Place asparagus in the pan with 2 oz. of the broth.
When it simmers, add the butter and, over low heat, keep moving the pan until all of the butter has melted and the asparagas is heated through.
Season with salt and pepper and serve the asparagus with its sauce.

BBQ Spiced Veal Chops
(8 servings)

Veal Chops

Ingredients

8	Veal chops, 10–12 oz. each
As needed	Giancarlo BBQ spice (from Chefnique)
As needed	Peanut oil

Method

In a mixing bowl, dredge chops with spice mix, coating evenly.
Add oil to sauté pan over high heat.
Add chops and brown well on both sides, about 3–4 minutes per side.
Remove the chops to a roasting pan with a rack, and finish in a 350° oven until desired doneness.

Spiced Sauce for Veal Chops

Ingredients

2 cups	Beef broth
4 oz.	Your favorite BBQ sauce
1 oz.	Mushroom soy sauce
To taste	Black pepper
6	Whole cloves
2	Bay leaves
3 sprigs	Fresh thyme
1 tsp.	Ground cumin
As needed	Roux or sauce thickener
	Note: For roux, melt 3 tbsp. butter in a saucepan. Add 3 tbsp. flour and mix well with a wooden spoon. Cook, stirring, for 2–3 minutes over low heat.
To taste	Salt and pepper

Method

Combine all ingredients and simmer for 30–45 minutes.
Strain stock and place back on the stove.
Add 1/2 cup of the stock to roux and create a smooth paste; add remaining stock, whisking well.
Simmer 3–4 minutes and adjust seasoning.
Serve 2–3 oz. over each veal chop.

Peach Compote
(2 cups)

Ingredients

3 cups	Fresh peaches, peeled and sliced
3 oz.	Sugar
¹/₂ cup	Balsamic vinegar
¹/₂ cup	Peach nectar
2 oz.	Sweet butter

Method

Toss peach slices with sugar and vinegar; let sit.

Combine marinade and nectar in a saucepan; bring to a boil.

Add peaches and simmer on low heat until almost tender, about 30–45 minutes.

Use to garnish the BBQ spiced veal chops (previous recipe) or your favorite grilled pork and veal recipes.

Chef José's Sports House Garlic Mashed Potatoes with Calabaza Squash in Plantain Bundles
(6 servings)

Ingredients

2 lbs.	Yukon Gold potatoes
1 tbsp.	Virgin olive oil
3 oz.	Sweet butter
5 cloves	Garlic, peeled and minced
1 cup	Heavy cream
3 tbsp.	Butter diced
To taste	Salt and pepper
1 small	Calabaza squash, cooked and diced
As needed	Plantain wrappers

Note: Plantain wrappers can be purchased in Chinese, Vietnamese, and Mexican markets.

Method

In a saucepan, cover potatoes in cold water, bring to boil, cover, and cook until tender.

Drain, let cool slightly, then peel and rice the potatoes twice. Keep warm.

Melt butter in pan with oil, and cook garlic until lightly brown.

Add cream; reduce to half.

Place cream mixture in blender and purée.

Fold in cream mixture and squash with riced potatoes; season with salt and pepper.

Lay out wrappers and fill with potato/squash mixture (or serve as is if preferred).

Fold into square bundles and finish in low oven.

Mind Over Matter

$\mathcal{M}$y experience as an apprentice in the 1984 Culinary Olympics was an inspiration, and it led me to continue entering culinary competitions. I worked hard upon my return, and entered many shows and categories, including pastry. I paid some dues along the way with bronze and silver medals, until the day I finally received my first American Culinary Federation gold medal.

The ACF medals are the toughest to garner for several reasons. One is that only certified judges who went through the process and won a certain number of gold medals themselves are allowed to judge. Second, the ACF does not hand out first, second, and third place prizes. They use a point system based on quality and craftsmanship, among other things. This system means you compete against yourself first. For example, there could be six chefs in the same category and all six could get gold medals if all the work was of gold-medal quality. The medal scores then are used to determine placement or special awards.

One time I entered two categories in one show, working endless hours all week, staying up 38 straight hours on the weekend before the show. The work paid off; I received two ACF gold medals for my work and best of show.

During the early fall of 1986, I received a call from Chef Helmut Hamann of Germany. He asked whether I wanted to try out for the 1988 ACF Culinary Team of New York. He said Chef Fritz and he had spoken about my hard work in 1984 and the progress I was making on the culinary competition circuit. He told me the try-outs would be in New York at the big hotel and restaurant show sponsored by one of the oldest chef associations, the Société Culinaire Philanthropic.

This was a huge opportunity for me, and I only had two months to get ready and plan my category. I practiced weekly and consulted every person I knew on my food and ideas. I also recruited some good help to assist during the week and to help me get everything to New York.

The week before the event, I worked on my centerpieces for the table: an eagle made out of salt dough and a chocolate lion. Then the week came to start the food preparation. I worked out of the corporate office and kitchens of TrustHouse Forte, my employer at the time.

The preparation was going well; I had drawings for everything, brand new silver the company had purchased for me, and china. Our table needed to be set by Saturday at 7:00 A.M. sharp.

On the Thursday before the show, I felt very weak and had a fever. This was not good. I had two days to go, and the last thing I needed was to be getting sick, especially since in all likelihood I would be up from Friday morning until Saturday afternoon. I managed to work quite a lot that day, but I was starting to drag and did not feel up to standing in the kitchen all night. There was so much left to do: food to cook, china to clean and polish, centerpieces to pack. After a bite of dinner, I decided to give everyone a break so I could take a short nap. I lay down on the floor in my office, took some medication, and slept for two hours.

When I got up I could barely stand. The chefs told me to go to a doctor and just pack it in. I did not look good at all, they said. No way. This was my big chance. A chance that if my work was good enough I could be on a team that would compete in the world's largest cookery competition. We must keep going. I worked until 1:00 A.M. on Friday, and then we left for some rest. Getting up later that morning was not easy; I could barely walk and felt like I should have stayed in bed. I went to the kitchen and got started. Everyone said I looked terrible, almost dead. The sad part was that I felt much worse than I looked!

It was a tough go, especially when 11:00 P.M. Friday came and we were not close to finishing. I was used to all-nighters, but not like this, not feeling this bad. I took breaks every 45 minutes or so, lying down on the floor. My throat was sore, and I could barely speak.

We started to pack, and I felt like I was truly on my last leg. I lay down in the van holding onto a silver platter and one of my pieces. I did my best to stay up during the ride to New York with all of my work. I was sweating like crazy but did not give in.

When we arrived we went inside. I received my table spot and set up with the help of my fellow chefs. I was about to collapse, but I knew I had to keep going just 10 to 20 more minutes. The table was just about done, and the people who came by all complimented me on how great it looked. The salt dough eagle was perched over the platter, and the food was some of the best work I had ever done.

We were taking pictures when Chef Hamann came by. He looked at me and said, "You look like you have seen a ghost." I was still sweating, and I was as white as one can get. I could not talk much; it hurt just to breathe at that point. He complimented my table and said it looked very good and the potential for Germany was very good. That made me happy, but I could not stay any longer. I needed to get out and go collapse. I didn't know what was wrong, but I knew it was not good.

I was supposed to be in New York for the next four days visiting the show. My throat was so dry I could hardly swallow, and I had been up for the last 29 hours straight. The chefs dropped me off at the Westbury Hotel (my favorite hotel, owned by TrustHouse Forte, of course). I had been there many times for work and to dine and stay over for company business. They saw me come in and were distressed at how I looked; they rushed me upstairs and said they were going to get a doctor to look after me. I went to the room, showered, and somehow ordered hot chicken broth from room service.

I was in bed when the doctor showed up. He took my temperature, looked me over, spent a good deal of time looking down my throat, and shook his head. He took a blood test and said to get some sleep; he also lectured me on not taking care of myself and not getting help sooner.

I went right to sleep when he left, until the phone rang. It was the general manager. He said he needed to see me and asked if he could come up. Great, I thought. I am here sick and he wants to discuss business! But that wasn't what he wanted. He had just come from the pharmacy and the doctor's office for me. He said, "The good news is I have medicine for you. The bad news is you have mononucleosis. This is very serious; you could have really done yourself some harm."

The doctor's orders were for plenty of rest, liquids, medication, soup broth, and bed rest for at least four days; end of story. I was not happy. I needed to go to the show; I needed to know how I did and whether I was part of the team for Germany. I also had meetings and business to attend to, but it was no use. I was to be bedridden for four days, assuming the medicine started to work.

I had calls those days and a visit from my boss, who said there was no announcement of the team, but those with whom he spoke loved the work and said it looked very good for me to earn one of the eight spots on the team. The president of TrustHouse even called to check on me and said not to worry about a thing and not to come back to work until I was 100% better.

I finally got back on my feet seven days later. The five-day stay at the Westbury was not such a bad thing. A week after I got back to work, I received a letter that said I was a member of the ACF Culinary Team of New York.

As I look back, I cannot believe that I worked with mono and did not realize how sick I was. It was then that I learned that our minds are extraordinary. When you are up against tough times, mind over matter really can make you be the best you can be!

Red Wine Dressing
(2 cups)

Ingredients

¼ cup	Merlot vinegar or aged red wine vinegar
¼ cup	Good red wine
1 tbsp.	Sugar
1 cup	Grapeseed oil
½ cup	Virgin olive oil
2 tbsp.	Basil, chopped
2 tbsp.	Sea salt

Method

Mix all ingredients together well. Use as a marinade for grilled meats or poultry, or as a dressing for your favorite salad.

White Anchovy Dressing
(2 cups)

Ingredients

2 tbsp.	Garlic, minced
6	White anchovies
1/2 cup	White balsamic vinegar
1 cup	Grapeseed oil
1/2 cup	Extra virgin olive oil
1 tsp.	Sugar
1 tbsp.	Sage, minced
1	Juice of 2 limes
To taste	Salt and pepper

Method

Mix all ingredients well in a blender.
Adjust consistency, if needed, with some cream or chicken broth.
Season with salt and pepper.
Serve over iceburg or romaine lettuce. This dressing is nice on a red onion and tomato salad as well.

Mayonnaise
(2 cups)

Ingredients

6	Egg yolks
2 tsp.	Kosher salt
1 pinch	White pepper
1 pinch	Old Bay seasoning
1–2 tbsp.	White balsamic vinegar or white wine vinegar
3 cups	Olive oil blend

Method

Season egg yolks with half of the vinegar, and lightly blend with blending stick.

Very slowly add oil while beating.

After mayonnaise starts to thicken, add remaining vinegar and season with salt and pepper.

Mayonnaise Variations

For saffron mayonnaise, add 2 tbsp. saffron water.

For garlic mayonnaise, add 2–3 tbsp. roasted garlic puree.

For basil mayonnaise, substitute 1 cup of basil oil for 1 of the cups of olive oil blend and add 3 tbsp. of finely chopped basil.

Ragù à la Bolognese
(1 quart)

Ingredients

1/2 cup	Extra virgin olive oil
1/2 cup	Small onions, diced small
1/4 cup	Celery, peeled and diced small
1/2 cup	Carrots, peeled and diced small
2 oz.	Prosciutto di Parma, finely diced
1/2 cup	Fresh chicken livers, finely chopped
1 lb.	Ground chuck
1 lb.	Ground pork
To taste	Salt and pepper
1/2 cup	Dry red wine
1/2 cup	Milk, hot
1/2 cup	Beef broth
1/2 cup	Tomatoes, diced
16 oz.	Tomato sauce

Method

Heat oil in pan with heavy bottom over medium heat.
Add onions and sauté until soft.
Add celery and carrot and cook for 3–5 minutes.
Add prosciutto and chicken livers; cook, stirring with wooden spoon, until meat is just cooked.
Crumble chuck and pork into pot; season with salt and pepper.
Break up meat and cook until tender, not brown.
Stir in wine, deglaze, and cook 2–3 minutes.
Reduce heat, add hot milk, and cook until evaporated.
Add broth, tomatoes, and tomato sauce and simmer 2–3 hours.

Stuffed Breast of Veal
(8 servings)

Ingredients

1	Veal breast, bone in, 4$^{1}/_{2}$–5$^{1}/_{2}$ lbs.
As needed	Olive oil
4 oz.	Veal bacon, diced
1 oz.	Sweet butter
2 oz.	Onions, diced
3 cloves	Garlic, sliced
12	Cremini mushrooms, sliced
$^{1}/_{4}$ cup	Parsley, chopped
1 tbsp.	Sage, chopped
To taste	Salt and pepper
10 oz.	Italian bread, diced
2 oz.	Milk
1	Egg
2 tbsp.	Extra virgin olive oil
1$^{1}/_{2}$ pts.	Veal stock
2	Bay leaves
4 sprigs	Fresh thyme
1	Onion, diced
4	Carrots, cut on bias
3 oz.	Fennel, diced
3 oz.	Celery, bias cut
12 small cloves	Garlic, peeled
2 oz.	Cold butter, diced
6	Plum tomato quarters, seeded and peeled

Method

Debone and prep veal breast for stuffing. Reserve bones and trimmings.
Heat a pan and render bacon with a touch of oil.
Add butter, onions, garlic, and mushrooms; cook until soft.
Fold in herbs and season with salt and pepper.
In a bowl, mix egg with milk.
Pour over bread; add olive oil.
Let sit 30 minutes.
Fold in cooked items.
Stuff breast with stuffing; secure with twine.
Place bones and trimmings in a roasting pan. Place breast on rack. Roast at 350° until tender, basting frequently with stock.
Remove veal; add remaining stock, bay leaf, and thyme, and simmer.
Sauté all vegetables except tomatoes.
Add to stock and simmer until tender.
Finish with some butter and add tomatoes.
Slice meat; serve with the sauce of vegetables, olive oil, and potatoes.

Chef Diesel

*W*hen competing in the world's largest culinary show, it is important to make trips prior to the event to ensure that all arrangements are taken care of. You will be performing in a different country, and a different language will be spoken. Many things need to be in order before your team's arrival—contracts signed for hotel rooms, vans rented, food shopped for and stored, meals arranged, and so forth.

In 2000, a dear chef friend and colleague from Germany came with the team as a liaison. His hard work and assistance were really an asset to the team. He was a German master chef and an American certified master chef, and he spoke fluent German and English. His mother and family still lived in Germany and had worked there for many years. They all worked hard to get the team whatever we needed.

After a great trip and a successful competition, with the United States finishing sixth over all with four gold medals, one silver, and one best in the world award for our cold table, we headed home.

The following year, Chef Buchner, my German friend, was competing with our team. He had been so excited to be part of the 2000 team, and now he would be back in 2004 as a cooking chef. In short, all went well for him, and he made the national team.

We both went on a trip to Erfurt and Frankfurt, Germany, in the fall of 2003 to arrange logistics for the show the following year. We met the chefs, booked the hotel rooms, and did all we had to do. We ate some great food, visited great markets, and did some great shopping as well.

The day came to leave Erfurt and head to Frankfurt. We were to meet with the president of the German Chefs Federation at his office and then have dinner. As we headed out for our three-hour plus trip, Chef Buchner said we needed gas. He pulled into one station and said that they did not have what we needed. I did not give this any thought. He went to the next station, got out and pumped the gas. After a few minutes I heard some mumbling and not-so-nice words from Chef Buchner. It seems Chef put petrol in the diesel gas tank of the rental car we were driving.

This was not good at all. Some men came out yelling in German and waving their arms and hands. We sat for a while; cell phones were used and advice given. All this trouble with a chef who was German, spoke German, read German, and was supposed to keep us non-Germans out of these kinds of messes!

Well, a tow truck was coming; they needed to take the tank out and drain it. The chances of making my meeting were not looking good. In fact, an hour went by and my New York-Italian personality was not happy. I had Chef Buchner call the dealer about the tow truck. They were waiting for the truck to get back from another run, and then they would send it to get us. After a ridiculous amount of time, the truck came and took us to the dealer. Perhaps we still could make it in time.

The driver, who we had never met before in our lives, had coffee with us while we waited and talked up a storm, giving us a geographic lesson on the places he had visited in the United States. No wonder it took him two hours to get to every poor stranded car! An hour and a half later I figured we are ready to go. Three men in blue overalls walked by, pushing our car, smiling, and just going about life as we became later for our meeting. They told us this happens all the time. Well, if this gas mix-up happens all the time, one would think that the nozzle or tank would be designed so it couldn't happen! A money-making racket, I figured.

Chef Buchner mentioned how glad he was that I did not speak German or it could have been a long day for us. (I am convinced New York urgency such as mine does not exist anywhere else.) We finally left, 300-plus Euros later, and headed to Frankfurt to at least have dinner with the president of the German Chefs Federation.

After this adventure, Chef Buchner became known as Chef Diesel to all of us who still love him so. Still, it does teach me that when in Rome even bringing a Roman does not mean you can do what they do!

Fränkische Bratwurst
(the one from my home town)
(8 bratwursts)

Ingredients

6 oz.	Beef chuck
10 oz.	Pork shoulder
16 oz.	Pork belly, fresh

Seasoning for each 2 lbs. of meat:

20 g	Salt
2 g	White pepper
1/2 g	Mace
1/2 g	Ginger, ground
3 g	Marjoram
1/2 g	Allspice
1/4 g	Garlic, chopped

Method

Cut meat into strips.
Mix with seasonings and chill well.
Grind through the 5 mm plate of a meat grinder.
Mix ground meat well until all seasonings are mixed in evenly.
Fill into small hog casings and form 3 1/2-oz. links.
Sauté in a little fat until golden and cooked through.

Sauerkraut
(the real thing)
(1 pound)

Ingredients

2 oz.	Vegetable oil
3 oz.	Onion, diced
4 oz.	Bacon, diced
2 lbs.	Savoy cabbage, thinly shredded
4 oz.	White wine
1 pt.	Vegetable or chicken broth
1	Spice sachet (include caraway seeds, bay leaves, juniper berry, and crushed peppercorns)
2 oz.	Sugar
4 oz.	Potato, peeled
To taste	Salt and white pepper

Method

Sauté onion and bacon in oil.
Add cabbage.
Add half of the wine, broth, sachet, and sugar.
Cover and braise in oven.
Grate potato and mix with remaining wine.
Add potato to kraut after $2/3$ cooking time.
Continue to cook until kraut is tender.
Remove sachet and season with salt and pepper.

Chevy Chase Crab Cakes
with Spicy Rémoulade Sauce
(eight 4-ounce cakes)

Crab Cakes

Ingredients

10 oz.	Mayonnaise
2 tbsp.	Parsley, chopped
2 tbsp.	Spice de Cosette seasoning
1 pinch	Cajun seasoning
2 tsp.	Worchestershire sauce
	Juice of 1 lemon
2 tsp.	Dijon mustard
2 lbs.	Picked lump crabmeat
3 oz.	Ritz Crackers, crushed

Method

Combine first seven ingredients to make a sauce.
Fold in the crabmeat and cracker crumbs.
Form into desired-size cakes and sauté gently in clarified butter until golden brown on each side.

Spicy Rémoulade Sauce

Ingredients

900 g	Mayonnaise
240 g	Ketchup
120 g	Capers, finely chopped
20 g	Anchovies, finely chopped
40 g	Green onions (green part), finely chopped
160g	Dijon mustard
100 g	Red wine vinegar
60 g	Paprika
40 g	Fresh parsley, minced
50 g	Prepared horseradish

30 g	Hot red pepper purée (cooked dried peppers)
10 g	Garlic, minced
40 g	Lemon juice
To taste	Salt and black pepper

Method

Mix all ingredients in a large bowl and let rest for 3 hours. Serve with the crab cakes.

Cumin-Dusted Beef Flank Steak with Ropa Vieja (Pulled Beef), Latin Vegetables, and Roasted Garlic-Cilantro Demi-Glace
(8 servings)

Rolled Flank Steak

Ingredients

1½ lb.	Flank steak, butterflied and square cut for rolling
As needed	Ground cumin
As needed	Granulated garlic
As needed	Salt
As needed	Ground white pepper
2 oz.	Parsley, washed and trimmed
2 oz.	Vegetable oil
	Butcher's string

Method

Remove fat and silverskin.

Trim flank steak to square ends; it should be approximately 12 inches in length.

Reserve trim for Ropa Vieja in following recipe.

Butterfly the flank steak and rub with vegetable oil.

Season with cumin, granulated garlic, salt, and ground white pepper.

Distribute washed and trimmed parsley over the flank steak, roll the steak, and tie with butcher's string.

Rub exterior with oil and repeat seasoning procedure.

Pan roast rolled flank steak.

Finish in 375° oven for 10–15 minutes.

Ropa Vieja (Pulled Beef)

Ingredients

1 lb.	Flank steak trim, reserved from Rolled Flank Steak recipe
1	Green pepper
1	Yellow pepper
1	Red pepper
1/2 qt.	Beef stock, reduced to half
1 oz.	Tomato paste
1 oz.	Vegetable oil
To taste	Salt
To taste	Ground white pepper

Method

Place reserved beef flank steak trim in pan with beef stock.
Bring to a boil and simmer until tender.
Take beef out and cool.
Add tomato paste to remaining beef stock and reduce to half.
Thicken sauce, if needed, and reserve.
Remove seeds from peppers and cut in julienne.
Cut cooked cooled flank steak into 2- or 3-inch lengths and pull into thin strips.
Quickly sauté julienne peppers in vegetable oil.
Add beef and sauce, heat, and adjust seasoning.

Demi-Glace

Ingredients

1 oz.	Butter
1 oz.	Carrots, chopped
1 oz.	Celery, chopped
2 oz.	Onion, chopped
1	Bay leaf
1 sprig	Thyme
1/4 oz.	Tomato purée
4 oz.	Red wine
2 qts.	Brown stock
To taste	Salt
1 oz.	Roasted garlic purée
1/2 oz.	Cilantro

Method

Sauté mirepoix (carrots, celery, and onion) in butter.
Add tomato purée and cook until vegetables are tender.
Deglaze with wine, add brown stock, simmer, and reduce to half.
Strain, bind with starch if necessary, and add thyme and salt to taste.
Add roasted garlic purée.
Add cilantro at serving time.

Latin Vegetables

Ingredients

1 lb.	Yucca
1 pinch	Achiote paste
To taste	Salt
To taste	Ground white pepper
1 ear	Corn, shucked, roasted, and cut off cob
1 oz.	Celery, diced small
1 oz.	Carrot, diced small
1 oz.	Scallion, sliced thin
To taste	Salt
To taste	Ground white pepper
1 oz.	Vegetable oil
4 oz.	Manioc flour, course
1gal.	Vegetable oil, for frying
1 lb.	Calabaza squash
1 lb.	Chayote squash, sliced
1 lb.	Asparagus tips, medium (90 tips)
1 cup	Chicken stock
2 oz.	Butter
To taste	Salt and pepper
To taste	Sugar

Method

For Stuffed Yucca Rounds:

Boil peeled yucca until tender. Remove fibers if present.

Mash and mix with achiote paste.

Season with salt and pepper.

Spread on a sheet pan lined with plastic wrap 3/8" to 1/4" thick, and chill completely.

Sauté corn kernels, celery, carrots, and scallions in vegetable oil.

Season to taste; remove and chill.

Cut chilled, mashed yucca into 4" rounds and dampen edges with water.

Place 1 oz. of vegetable mixture in each yucca round and fold in half to seal.

Form stuffed yucca rounds into oblong shapes, dampen with water, and roll in coarse manioc flour.

Fry stuffed yucca rounds in 360° oil until crisp.

For the Remaining Vegetables:

Peel and seed calabaza squash. Cut into large dice. Reserve trimmings.

Boil a little chicken stock; add tournée squash and some butter, cook until tender, and season.

Blanch chayote squash, chill and place on sheet pan in a shingled fan arrangement, season.

Blanch asparagus tips, chill, heat with butter, and season for serving.

Sweat squash trimmings.

Add some chicken stock and cook until tender.

Purée, add butter, and season.

Plate Assembly

Place chayote squash fan on plate and top center edge with some squash purée.

Lay the tournée squash on the squash purée.

Place stuffed yucca round beside the vegetables.

Portion ropa vieja toward center of the plate, and top with a slice of rolled flank steak.

Place asparagus tip next to meat.

Finish the plate with the sauce.

Red Onion Cheese Tart
(two 9-inch tarts)

Tart Shell Dough

Ingredients

1 cup	Butter
1¼ cups	All-purpose flour
1 tsp.	Salt
1	Egg
3 oz. (approx.)	Water

Method

Cut butter into flour (leave butter pieces larger than peas).
Add egg and enough water just to combine.
Wrap with plastic wrap, and refrigerate for 24 hours.
Roll out dough and line two 9-inch pie shells.
Prick holes in shells and bake in 350° oven until lightly browned.

Cheesecake Filling

Ingredients

1 cup	Port Salút, rind removed, room temperature.
1½ cups	Cream Cheese, room temperature
½ cup	Goat cheese, room temperature
2 tbsp.	Basil, chopped
1 tsp.	Granulated garlic
½ tsp.	Freshly ground black pepper
1 tsp.	Taste of Roma spice mix
4 tbsp.	Tomatoes, diced
1 cup	Sour cream
4	Eggs
¼ cup	Mozzarella cheese, shredded

Method

Mix Port Salút in mixing bowl with paddle until softened.
Slowly add cream cheese until thoroughly combined. Scrape bowl well.
Add goat cheese, basil, garlic, pepper, Roma spice, and tomatoes, then sour cream. Scrape bowl well.
Add eggs slowly, scraping bowl after each addition.
Fold in mozzarella cheese.

Onions

Ingredients

2 large	Red onions
As needed	White vinegar
3 tbsp.	Sugar

Method

Slice onions thin, place in pan with vinegar, and bring to a boil.
Drain off vinegar and let onions cool.

To Finish

Fill pre-baked shells with cheesecake batter. Sprinkle onions over top.
Bake in 300° oven until firm (approximately 40 minutes).

Reader's Notes and Thoughts

It Takes Time to Win

*B*ack in March of 1999, I was appointed to be the team captain and manager of the ACF Culinary Team USA 2000. It was a long-time dream of mine to represent the chefs of the United States and lead the only national team from the United States to the German Culinary Olympics *(Kochkunst In Bildern)*. This event, as mentioned in my apprenticeship tales, was the show of shows for chefs.

Before this, however, in May of 1999, the team was to compete in a show called the Culinary Classic at the restaurant show in Chicago. This event is held every three years and usually brings 8 to 12 teams from Europe to compete for the Culinary Classic Cup. We would compete in Basel, Switzerland, in November of the same year and would have 12 months to get ready for Germany.

This was going to be the largest challenge of my competitive culinary career, because much was expected from the U.S. teams. Our success from 1976 until the present had shown the Europeans that food in the United States and the chefs who prepared it were of good quality—equal to what chefs in other countries cooked. In fact, in 1980, 1984, and 1988 the team won gold medals in the hot kitchen category, and they won the championship in 1988.

My challenge was to choose five out of nine chefs (along with myself) to make up the six-person national team. The remaining four would be on a regional team that would compete in a buffet program only. We had to act fast because in two months our first international competition would be starting on our home turf.

In a few weeks the team was assembled, and we started to prepare for the Culinary Classic. I would soon learn that managing and leading a team of talented chefs was much more involved than leading your own kitchen brigade.

The Culinary Classic was a learning experience for us. The first time out of the gate we performed well, but not at the level of a national team. We placed fourth, with two gold medals and two silvers. The devastating one was the silver medal in the hot kitchen competition, which was the toughest part of the program. The Swiss took first, and there we were, fourth in our own country.

We got past that, however, and prepared for Switzerland. It was a great show, and just to be in Switzerland representing the United States and our cuisine was an honor. We worked out of a private hospital in Switzerland, and we put in endless hours. I will never forget the morning of our cold buffet program and how we paid eight taxicabs to line up and drive only 10 to 15 miles per hour to ensure that our items got to the exhibit hall safely.

Things went much better in Basel. We still received a silver medal for our hot kitchen efforts, but we scored much higher than we had in Chicago, and we took three gold medals for our cold program. The icing on the cake, so to speak, was that we took a special award for first in the cold category out of 18 countries and finished fifth overall.

After the competition, I took a few days with my wife to enjoy Zurich and all the holiday and fall season had to offer. I felt much better than I had after the Chicago competition. Even though you learn in either case, it seemed better to win and perform well than to lose.

After taking the holiday time, we had to get ready for the Big Daddy of all culinary shows: the German Culinary Olympics. This would be tough. The competition in Germany would consist of 28 teams and some of the finest chefs in the world. Many of the teams were very seasoned and had been together since 1996. This would be their second showing, and they had eight years' experience in cooking together. We had been cooking together for only six months.

After months of practicing and getting ready, we left for the big show in Erfurt, Germany. The trip itself was amazing, except for the eight-hour bus ride from Frankfurt to Erfurt! We did stop at a wonderful rest area, but the two women in back cooking all of this home-style, delicious food almost fell to the floor when 25 of us walked in and cleaned them out of everything they had cooked and more!

When we arrived in Erfurt, we checked into the hotel and went to visit the kitchen we were going to work in. The hospital and its crew were very good to us. They had us do a special American-style lunch for their VIPs and took pictures of all of us with the hospital chef and the director. The women in the kitchen, including the little red-headed salad girl, took a liking to some team members. The salad girl had a crush on my colleague, Chef Buchner (a.k.a. Chef Diesel), but that's another story.

Five days before show time, we began working hard. The pastry program was very important and took much work due to the detail, craftsmanship, and artistic talent needed. As always, not everything went well. We lost our silver tray for the cold meat display, the marzipan fruits all had to be redone to look real, and so on. The day came for the cold food competition, so we set out for the hall, getting ready at 5:00 A.M. (We had until 8:00 A.M. to be ready and have all chefs clear of the table area.)

The chefs were all trying to get the food displayed and in order before the judges started. The pastry chefs worried me a bit since the time was ticking away and they were not finished with their set-up. Chef Tom Vaccaro, who was the national team's pastry coach, assured me that all was well. (Chef Tom is a huge pastry talent and the Executive Pastry Chef of the Trump Plaza Hotel in Atlantic City.) The display of blown and pulled sugar, cocoa paintings, and chocolate sculptures was sure to impress the judges.

I double-checked to ensure that all was in order and things were going well. We had signage for the food in both German and English. I started to hustle everyone to start cleaning as 8:00 A.M. drew closer. As I rushed to make sure that everyone else was moving and the other support help were away from the table, I noticed that the pastry chefs were still working on the display and it did not look like they were going to be on time.

This did not make me happy, and instead of taking a calm approach, I started to put more pressure on them. I was all over them to move it; they had enough time to do this; they were the ones here first, and they were going to cost us points.I kept at it and saw that they were not appreciative of my pushing. Just then my pastry coach and friend Chef Vaccaro looked up at me as calm as I have ever seen a person under the circumstances and said, "Chef, it takes time to win."

I was speechless. I did not no how to rebuke this and just gave him a puzzled look. He gave me a smirky smile in return.

It takes time to win. I have never forgotten that phrase and how it lightened up the moment and helped me keep calm. It shows you that even in the chaos of the moment a cool, calm head will always brighten the day.

The team went on to do very well; we scored three gold medals for our cold buffet, a silver for our hot kitchen, and first place in the world for our plated food category on the buffet. We finished sixth overall out of 28 teams.

We went on to Scotland six months later and received four gold medals in every category, including the hot kitchen; we finished third overall. We also returned to the Culinary Classic in May of 2003 in Chicago and swept the competition, winning the Culinary Classic Cup.

We may eat hamburgers and hot dogs in the United States, but we know good food as well and how to take the time to win!

Blood Orange Curd Tarts
(4 servings)

Tart Shells

Ingredients

5 oz.	Pastry flour
2 tbsp.	Sugar
Pinch	Salt
4 oz.	Unsalted butter
2 tbsp.	Cold water
1	Egg yolk
1 oz.	Pine nuts, chopped and toasted
2 tbsp.	Butter, diced

Method

Combine flour, salt, and sugar and cut butter into this mixture.
Add egg yolks, nuts, and enough water to bring dough together; do not overwork dough.
Chill for 1 hour.
Roll dough out to ⅛ inch thickness and place in four 3-inch tart shells.
Blind bake in a 350° oven until done (15–20 minutes).
Set aside to cool.

Note: *Blind bake* means to bake crust until lightly browned and finished without a filling.

Filling

Ingredients

6	Egg yolks
6 oz.	Sugar
4 oz.	Blood orange juice
1	Blood orange zest, grated

Method

Combine egg yolks, sugar, and juice.

Cook over a hot water bath, stirring constantly.

When very thick, remove from the heat and stir in small pieces of butter and zest.

Stir until butter is completely melted.

Pour curd into tart shells and chill until set.

Serve with whipped cream.

Autumn Pear and Spice Soufflé
(8 servings)

Ingredients

4	Pears, peeled and diced
2 tbsp.	Sugar
$1/2$ tsp.	Cinnamon
To taste	Lemon juice
To taste	Butter
32 oz.	Milk
8 oz.	All purpose flour
10 oz.	Sugar
4	Whole eggs
12	Egg yolks
1 tbsp.	Cinnamon
$1/2$ tsp.	Nutmeg
$1/4$ tsp.	Clove
12	Egg whites

Method

Butter and sugar 8 large soufflé cups.
Sauté pears in butter and add 2 tbsp. sugar, $1/2$ tsp. cinnamon, and lemon juice to taste.
Make sure pears are fully cooked.
Strain fruit and divide among the soufflé cups.
Set aside.
Heat milk to a scald.
Mix whole eggs, flour, and 10 oz. sugar together.
Temper milk into egg mixture.
Return mixture to the heat and stir continuously with a wooden spoon; mixture will thicken.
Continue to stir until the mixture is smooth and pulls away from the sides of the pot.
Let cool slightly.
Mix in the spices.
Mix in the egg yolks, 2 at a time.
Beat the egg whites to soft peaks.
Fold the egg whites into the soufflé batter.
Portion the batter into the soufflé cups.

Bake at 375° for 45 minutes.
Dust with powdered sugar, and serve immediately.
Serve Cinnamon Cream Anglaise on the side (recipe follows).

Cinnamon Cream Anglaise

Ingredients

16 oz.	Milk
1/2	Vanilla bean, scraped
6	Egg yolks
4 oz.	Sugar
1/2 tsp.	Cinnamon

Method

Scald milk with scraped vanilla bean.
Mix egg yolks and sugar together.
Temper milk into egg mixture and continue to cook until the custard coats the back of a spoon (180° to 185°).
Add the cinnamon, strain, and keep warm.
Be careful not to break the custard.
Serve on the side with the Autumn Pear and Spice Soufflé.

Banana Cream Chiboust
(4 servings)

Ingredients

4	Tartlet molds lined with puffed pastry (unbaked)
2	Bananas, sliced
2	Eggs
1 cup	Whipping cream
2 oz.	Sugar

Method

Place the banana slices in the tartlet shells.
Mix together the remaining ingredients and pour over the bananas.
Bake at 375° F until the custard is just set and the pastry is golden brown.

Chiboust

Ingredients

4 oz.	Egg yolks
1 oz.	Cornstarch
1 cup	Milk
4 oz.	Sugar
1 tsp.	Vanilla extract
1/2 oz.	Gelatin
2 tbsp.	Cold water
5 oz.	Egg whites
5 oz.	Sugar

Method

Combine the yolks, cornstarch, 2 oz. of the sugar, and enough milk to mix to a smooth paste.
Put remaining milk, 2 oz. sugar, and vanilla in a pan and bring to a boil.
Remove from heat and pour over the yolk mixture; combine well.
Pour back into the pan and reboil, stirring constantly so the custard does not burn on the base of the pan.
Remove from heat.
Place the water in a small bowl, sprinkle the gelatin over the water, and allow the gelatin to be absorbed.

Add the gelatin to the custard (which should still be hot) and stir in so the gelatin dissolves.

Cover with plastic wrap directly on the surface and place in the refrigerator; cool until tepid (not cold).

Combine egg whites and 5 oz. sugar and whip to a soft peak.

Fold the egg mixture into the tepid custard and blend carefully.

Assembly

Pipe the chiboust onto the baked banana custard.

Sprinkle with granulated sugar and, using a torch, heat the sugar so it caramelizes and forms a caramel crust on the chiboust.

Maple Apple Frangipane with Pecan Soufflé
(8 servings)

Frangipane

Ingredients

8 oz.	Almond paste
4 oz.	Butter
1 oz.	Sugar
2	Eggs, beaten
1/2 oz.	Flour
2	Granny Smith apples
3 oz.	Pure maple syrup

Method

Cream almond paste, butter, and sugar until smooth and creamy.
Gradually add the beaten eggs.
Fold in the flour.
Peel and finely slice the apples, toss in maple syrup.
Pipe the frangipane into the bottom of small cake forms (muffin tins can be used).
Fill with the sliced apples.
Bake at 350° until golden brown, approximately 20 minutes.

Pecan Frozen Soufflé

Ingredients

16 oz.	Whipped cream
3	Egg yolks
1 tbsp.	Pecan flavoring
1	Egg
6 oz.	Sugar
4 oz.	Pecans, chopped

Method

Combine egg yolks, flavoring, egg, and sugar in a mixing bowl.
Place in a double boiler over hot water.
Using a whisk, stir constantly until lukewarm.
Place the bowl on a mixer and whip until cool. The mixture should be at ribbon stage (thick and foamy) when cool.
Fold in the whipped cream.
Fold in the pecans.
Pour into molds or a terrine form.
Cover and freeze.

Assembly

Turn the apple frangipane out of the molds with the help of a knife.
Put on a dessert plate and dust with powdered sugar.
Place the soufflé mold in warm water; turn the soufflé out and place next to the frangipane.

Chocolate Mousse in Tuiles
(10 servings)

Ingredients

10 oz.	Chocolate, semisweet
1½ oz.	Butter
5	Egg yolks, pasteurized
2 oz.	Sugar
5	Egg whites, pasteurized
1 fluid oz.	Dark rum or vanilla (to taste)
8 fluid oz.	Heavy cream, whipped
10	Tuiles (cup-shaped wafers)

Method

Combine chocolate and butter; melt over a water bath.
Whip egg yolks and half the sugar to full volume.
Whip egg whites and the remaining sugar to full volume.
Fold egg whites into egg yolks.
Fold butter-chocolate mixture into egg-sugar mixture.
Spoon evenly into tuiles. Garnish with whipped cream and strawberries
if desired.

Reader's Notes and Thoughts

Mark Ammerman 2004

The Beginning

I will never forget my first chef's job and the challenges that awaited me there. I was working at the Red Coach Grille, an upscale dining restaurant owned by Howard Johnson's. They had about 13 of these restaurants, all with banquet facilities and a famous salad bar. We had the second highest banquet business in the company. and we cooked a Sunday brunch.

The restaurant was nice, and we got to do many new things, especially with banquets. I worked for a Greek chef at the time named George. He was a burly, hard-working man who had been with the company for eight years. He promoted me to the position as his sous-chef and took me under his wing to teach me the many things he had learned in his years in the business.

The restaurant had a staff of 22 in the kitchen, and we used an actual wood-burning grill to cook the steaks and chops. The crew included some strange characters who were pretty tough. (A few of them thought they should have got the sous-chef job instead of me.) I remember once when the chef had a huge fight with the broiler person, who walked out and came back 20 minutes later looking for Chef with a gun. I remember thinking that perhaps a new job was in order. The chef was not there, and the very upset broiler cook left after the police showed up. We never saw or heard from him again.

Two months after my promotion, a new general manager came in—a fairly young guy who was favored by the company and had many new ideas. This did not sit well with Chef, and from time to time they would have arguments on many subjects. As the holidays approached, the chef and general manager had a big blowout, and the chef was yelling in Greek. He then looked at me and said, "No young hot shot in a suit is going to tell me how to run a kitchen." He left his keys with me and said, "My best to you, and one day you may just make a fine chef."

The general manager called me into his office and said that I should take over for now since I was sous-chef, and he would decide at some point what to do. He went over his game plan with me, his philosophy for the restaurant and such. He called a meeting the next day to let everyone know what had happened and to tell them that I would run the kitchen.

The other cooks were not pleased, and I knew they would test me from time to time. I took to the job like a madman, cooking up new dishes, changing the banquet menus, and putting every ounce of energy that I had into the job. The corporate chef was a big help and supported me; he regarded me as a young son learning the ropes.

We did some great things, and our banquet business took off as the holidays approached. It was Thanksgiving, and we had a huge number of turkeys to prepare; we would serve more than 800 covers that day.

My first lesson as a chef was not to anger the staff when you really need them. The pastry chef was creating a marvelous turkey out of cake and marzipan, and he left it near the ovens. I was running around frenetically and went to make sure that all the turkeys were cooking. I saw this big brown bird on the table in a roasting pan, quickly muttered something about the cooks not doing their job, and threw it into the oven.

I was in the office checking the ordering when I heard a loud yell and some very nasty words. I ran to the kitchen to find the pastry chef in an uproar. The oven door was open, and the cooks all around him were laughing. As I went near to calm him down, he started yelling "Chef, some stupid idiot placed my turkey cake in the oven!"

I looked in the oven and there was a turkey-shaped cake with frosting all melted and turning into quite a mess. I realized what I had done. I turned to tell him, but he kept going on, "What person in this kitchen with such a lack of brains would dare do this!"

I said, "Well, that would be me, the chef."

Everyone cleared the kitchen, some still smirking. The pastry chef's mouth opened, and he started to say, "Chef, I did not know! Chef, I did not mean . . . ."

I took him into the office and first apologized and said his work was so good that I could not tell that it wasn't a real turkey as I walked through. He just sat there and said, "Well, the damage is done. My cake is ruined; the crew saw me say things I shouldn't have, and they sure know it was you who put it in the oven, so I must go. I will go bake elsewhere in a better kitchen than this one."

Right then I knew that I had blown it. I knew the respect of the crew would need to be won back. The pastry chef left and did not say a word to anyone. Most of the crew figured I fired him for his outburst, which was not a bad thing.

The rest of the holidays went very well, and after the new year the general manager gave me the job on a permanent basis. So began my career as a chef. In the beginning, as with so many things, there were many growing pains. I have learned, however, that without mistakes you cannot become better; you cannot learn what you need to in life.

I learned that surrounding yourself with a talented and hard-working kitchen brigade was a key to any chef's success, and I learned that this was just the beginning of what was to come. The journey had not ended just because I was a chef. This was just the beginning of a long trip that would take some detours but was not destined to end.

Wild Mushroom Chili
(8–10 servings)

Ingredients

5 oz.	Olive oil
6	Shallots, diced
4 cloves	Garlic, sliced thin
3 lbs.	Mixed wild mushrooms, chopped
1 cup	Tomatoes, chopped
1/2 cup	Red wine
1/2 qt.	Chicken broth or mushroom broth
1 lb.	Red or white beans, cooked
2 tbsp.	Oregano
3 tbsp.	Ground cumin
1 large	Smoked chili, diced
1/4 cup	Mushroom soy
2 tbsp.	Chili powder
3 tsp.	Cinnamon
3 tbsp.	Butter

Method

Sauté garlic and shallots in olive oil until soft.
Add mushrooms and cook for 12–15 minutes.
Add tomatoes and wine and cook until all liquid is evaporated,
5–10 minutes.
Add broth and remaining items.
Simmer for 30 minutes.
Adjust seasoning as needed, and serve over rice if desired.

Caponata
(8–12 servings)

Ingredients

2 lbs.	Eggplant, peeled and diced
4	Red bell peppers, diced large
1/2 cup	Kalamata olives, split
1/2 cup	Green olives, split
3 oz.	Olive oil
1/2 cup	Extra virgin olive oil
2 tsp.	Red pepper, crushed
4 tbsp.	Garlic, minced
2 oz.	Balsamic vinegar

Method

Salt eggplant and let stand 2 hours on a cloth.
Rinse eggplant and pat dry.
In a large sauté pan, sear eggplant, red bell peppers, and olives in 3 oz. olive oil on high heat; place in bowl.
Sweat garlic and crushed red pepper in 1/2 cup hot olive oil; pour over vegetables.
Add balsamic vinegar, toss well, and chill.

Tomato Confit
(16 pieces)

Ingredients

4	Plum tomatoes, peeled and seeded
2 cloves	Garlic, sliced thin
6 oz.	Olive oil
1 tbsp.	Cumin
1/2 tbsp.	Coriander
To taste	Kosher salt

Method

Cut tomatoes into quarters and place on a lightly oiled pan.
Season with cumin, coriander and salt.
Place 2–3 slices of garlic on each tomato quarter.
Drizzle with oil.
Bake at 325° until soft but slightly firm.
Remove garlic; reserve.

Serve with chicken dishes, fish, or veal or toss with pasta or use as a garnish or vegetable.

Roasted Garlic Sauce

Ingredients

2 bulbs or 1 cup cloves	Garlic
1 oz.	Butter
1¹/₂ cups	White wine
2	Shallots, minced
3 cups	Heavy cream
To taste	Salt and pepper
2 tbsp.	Extra virgin olive oil

Method

Place garlic in a small pan, ³/₄ covered with chicken stock and butter.
Roast at 275° until cloves are tender.
Simmer wine and shallots in saucepan until about 1 oz. is left.
Place roasted garlic cloves into saucepan with wine and shallots; add cream.
Simmer until reduced in half.
Puree with hand blender or regular blender; strain.
Season with salt and pepper and extra virgin olive oil.

Pan-Seared Alaskan Salmon
(6–8 servings)

Ingredients

6–8 (3–4 oz. each)	Salmon filets, center cut
To taste	Kosher salt
To taste	Freshly ground black Tellicherry pepper
3/4 cup	Honey
1/2 cup	Virgin olive oil
	Juice of 2 limes
	Juice of 1 lemon
2 tbsp.	Fresh tarragon, minced

Method

Season each filet with salt and pepper.
Mix remaining items well, coat filets with marinade on each side.
Let sit for 20–30 minutes.
Pan sear until golden brown on each side (about 2–3 minutes).
Finish in 350° oven until just cooked in center.

Choucroute for Fish
(8 servings)

Ingredients

2 cups	High-quality sauerkraut, drained and rinsed well
5 pieces	Smoked bacon, matchbook cut
1 tbsp.	Peanut oil
1 small	Onion, medium dice
2 cloves	Garlic, sliced thin
1 tsp.	Caraway seeds
1/2 cup	White wine
1 cup	New potatoes, cooked and sliced
1 tbsp.	Parsley, chopped
To taste	Kosher salt
To taste	Black pepper, freshly ground
2 tbsp.	Sweet butter

Method

Render bacon in oil until crisp.
Add onion and garlic; cook until soft.
Add caraway seeds and deglaze pan with wine.
Add potato slices and parsley.
Season with salt and pepper.
Add butter, then sauerkraut, and mix well.
Add seasonings.
Serve hot.

Fragrant Fruit Rice Pilaf
(8 servings)

Spice Mix

Ingredients

$1/6$ oz.	Ground allspice
$1/6$ oz.	Cumin
$1/3$ oz.	Cardamom
1 tsp.	Saffron threads
To taste	Kosher salt

Method

Mix all items well, reserve.

Note: You can eliminate the saffron, or substitute the same amount of sweet curry or turmeric.

Pilaf

Ingredients

1 oz.	Olive oil
2 oz.	Butter
8 oz.	Onion, diced
2 cloves	Garlic, sliced
6 oz.	Carrot, diced
16 oz.	Rice
20 oz.	Vegetable broth
12 oz.	Pineapple juice

Method

Heat oil in pan.

Add butter, then onions and garlic.

Cook for 2–3 minutes.

Add carrot and cook until slightly brown.

Add spice mix and cook for 1–2 minutes longer.

Add rice and stir to coat.

Add broth and fruits.

Cover and bake in a 350° oven until rice is tender and absorbs the liquid, 12–15 minutes.

Garnish with toasted almonds and coconut.

Reader's Notes and Thoughts

From the Fire into the Pan

*T*his is a poem I wrote in 1996 after taking my master chef exam and looking at my career as a chef and where I wanted it to go next.

There I was—an apprentice learning to cook
It was then, and even now, that I read many a book.

I trained by day, I trained by night
To cook by the fire was my flight.

The chefs I have had were mentors to me, the ones who would spend the time to teach
The young eager cook, I was ready to seek the knowledge that they would bring—share, so to speak.

The journey was there for me to travel
Peeling, chopping, washing pots—whatever it took I would not unravel.

I learned all I could and did what I should
Into the fire I would go one day under the kitchen hoods.

I tried new things, I sought new ideas
On the way took some spills, but never did I fear.

The time was now, the moment had come to go into the fire and into the pan,
It was then being a chef would mean to be all I can.

Yes, into the fire and into the pan
It means you never look back, but never forget where you have come from again.

I cook with passion
I cook with love
I keep on learning
I keep the fire burning above.

You get up every day and never say when
Because soon enough it is into the fire again.

Yes into the fire and into the pan
It is my life, my passion; it is who I am.

Chef Edward G. Leonard, 1996

Thai Chicken Sandwich
(8 servings)

Ingredients

8 (6 oz. each)	Chicken breasts, trimmed
1 can	Coconut milk
3 tbsp.	Fresh ginger, grated
2 stalks	Lemon grass, chopped
2 tbsp.	Curry powder
1 oz.	Asian chili sauce
2 oz.	Peanut oil
1 tbsp.	Cilantro, chopped
1 tsp.	Kosher salt

Method

Mix all items well except lemon grass.
Place chicken in a pan and top with lemon grass.
Marinate with dressing for a minimum of 4 hours.
Coat grill with oil and grill chicken to mark on each side.
Finish in a 350° oven for 5–8 minutes with some of the marinade.
Serve on brioche loaf or French bread with your favorite peanut sauce and chopped coconut.

Surf & Turf
(4 servings)

Ingredients

14 oz.	Ribeye steaks with bone
To taste	Salt and pepper
3 tbsp.	Virgin olive oil
1 1/2 cups	Worcestershire sauce
1 1/2 cups	Smoky BBQ sauce
As needed	French fried onion rings, about 4–6 per person
12	Large shrimp, peeled and deveined
3 tbsp.	Sesame oil
2 oz.	Sesame seeds, toasted
1 tbsp.	Ginger, grated
1/2 cup	Red Hot sauce
2 oz.	Worcestershire sauce

Method

Marinate steak and shrimp with their respective ingredients for a minimum of 3 hours.

Take 1 cup of the marinade from the steak and bring to a boil on the stove.

Chargrill both the steak and the shrimp until desired doneness.

Spoon 2 tbsp. of marinade on each steak.

Top with French fried onion rings and place in salamander or hot oven until onion rings are toasted.

Assembly

Serve one steak and three shrimp on each platter with some sautéed spinach and carrots.

Sandwich Pan Bagnat Garfield
(6 servings)

Ingredients

3 cans (5 oz. each)	Chunk white tuna
3 cans	Chunk light tuna in olive oil
1 head	Romaine lettuce, chopped
6	Roma tomatoes, diced
2 small	Fennel bulbs, sliced very thin
3 cloves	Garlic, minced
1/2 cup	Black olives, pitted and sliced
6 oz.	Worcestershire sauce
1 tbsp.	Dijon mustard
2 tbsp.	Anchovy paste
4 oz.	Olive oil
To taste	Salt and pepper
6 oz.	BBQ sauce
6 oz.	Hellmann's mayonnaise
2 large loaves	French bread

Method

Drain tuna well and place in a bowl.

Chop romaine and reserve.

Mix Worcestershire sauce, mustard, anchovy paste, and olive oil well.

Place tomatoes, olives, fennel, and garlic in a bowl; toss with half the dressing and season.

Mix tuna with the other half of the dressing.

Toss romaine with BBQ sauce and mayonnaise.

Cut open bread loaves, hollow out, and fill with romaine, tuna, and salad mixture.

Let sit for 10 minutes.

Seafood Tomato Sauce
with Pasta and Crispy Shrimp
(6 servings)

Ingredients

4 oz.	Olive oil
6 oz.	Anchovies, minced, or anchovy paste
2 tsp.	Red pepper flakes
$^1/_2$ cup	Dry white wine
$^1/_2$ qt.	Tomato sauce
24	Small clams
24	Prince Edward Island mussels
1	Lobster, cleaned and chopped into 6 pieces, 4 from the tail and 4 from the claws
1 lb. (21/25 count)	Shrimp, peeled, breaded, and fried
1 cup	Seafood broth
3 tbsp.	Parsley, chopped
1 tsp.	Basil, chopped
1 tbsp.	Extra virgin olive oil
1 tbsp.	Butter
1 lb.	Spaghetti or linguine, cooked

Method

Sauté anchovy and pepper flakes in olive oil for 2–3 minutes.

Add white wine to pan and simmer until almost dry.

Add tomato sauce, clams, mussels, lobster, shrimp, and seafood broth to pan.

Simmer 10–15 minutes.

Add parsley and basil; finish with extra virgin olive oil and butter.

Toss with spaghetti or linguine and top each bowl with 2 deep-fried or pan-fried shrimp.

Georgia Pecan Delight
(8 servings)

Ingredients

1/2 lb.	Unsalted butter, room temperature
2 oz.	Confectioners' sugar
1 oz.	Dark brown sugar
6 oz.	Semisweet chocolate, melted and kept warm
6	Egg yolks, room temperature
1/2 oz.	Grand Marnier
6	Egg whites, room temperature
4 oz.	Sugar
6 oz.	Unflavored bread crumbs
8 oz.	Pecans, roasted and ground (reserve 2 oz. for garnish)

Garnish

Confectioners' sugar
Semisweet chocolate curls and shavings
Whipped cream flavored with rum
Strawberries, hulled and sliced
Reserved pecans

Method

Mix butter with sugars until well combined.
Add egg yolks gradually to chocolate until well combined.
Add Grand Marnier to chocolate mixture and mix well.
Combine the chocolate mixture and the butter mixture. Do not allow to get cold; work quickly.
Whip egg whites with 4 oz. of sugar until stiff.
Fold half of the egg whites into the chocolate base to lighten the product a bit.
Fold in the bread crumbs and 6 oz. of pecans.
Fold in the remaining egg whites; try not to deflate mixture.
Fill individual buttered molds with 5 oz. of pudding.
Place filled molds into a hotel pan and add hot water until it reaches halfway up the sides of the molds.
Cover entirely with foil and bake at 350° for 30–35 minutes.
Remove baked puddings from water bath and cool for at least 1 hour.

To remove pudding, gently press fingers around edges of molds to loosen; turn upside down and ease out.

Dust with confectioners' sugar in a decorative pattern.

Garnish with semisweet chocolate curls. Pipe with flavored whipped cream and sprinkle with pecans, chocolate shavings, and strawberry slices.

Note: I used 5-oz. oven-proof ceramic salad bowls as molds.

What the #@*#~ Is Quiche?

One good thing about being a chef is the opportunities you get to help out, plan events, and consult on occasions. A friend of mine had a big event coming up. He was new at the job and needed some help. He worked for a corporate operation, feeding employees and doing their special events. He had a winter festival coming up, and he wanted to impress everyone.

I went over right away to help him plan and get the ball rolling. We looked at all types of menu options and how to decorate the area and garnish the food. I said to him, "Quiche is becoming a big thing. People in the New York restaurants are serving it for lunch, brunch, and as a starter. We can be trendsetters and do a quiche bar featuring a variety of house-made quiches." He did not seem to mind this, and he thought doing something new and exciting would show his clients that they had a chef who knew his stuff.

I took some time off to help him prep and get ready for the big day. The place looked great. We worked around the clock and made some wonderful things. The menu for the festival was something like this:

Winter pumpkin soup with toasted pumpkin seeds

Seasonal selection of salads with dressings

Variety of house-made quiches with a tossed salad and poppy seed dressing

Grilled Croque Monsieur sandwiches

Roasted pear cakes and more

The client came in and was taken aback by the work and the display of food.

She then grabbed my buddy and spoke to him quietly in the corner. I said to myself, "Something must be going on here." He came back looking a bit puzzled and said that she loved everything but was concerned that the guests might not have enough substance, as she put it.

"Substance," I said. "What is she speaking of? Our quiches, salads, soups, and elegant sandwiches! Why, these people will go crazy for our efforts! They will be remembering this affair for some time after it is over. Be proud and let the people relish in our fine cuisine," I told him.

Little did I know I would be right. The doors opened and in came these big, burly men who looked as if they could eat a horse and then some. They walked up to my buddy and said, "Where is the real food? We are starved." It seems the special event was for a contractor as a thank you for all the work they had done for the company over the past year. In fact, there were more than 150 of these hungry "where's the beef" kind of customers standing around our buffet.

I started to help serve and took over the quiche station. One of the guys came up to me and said, "Where is the prime rib, Chef? Where is the meat course?" He was a bit on the large side, with hands that looked as if they could hold two basketballs each and make them pop. He must have been at least 6'3" and 300 pounds.

I looked up and said, "Well sir, there is no prime rib, but we do have a great selection of quiche that you can try."

"Quiche? Quiche?" He said this twice and stared at me in a not-so-friendly manner. Then in the deepest voice I have ever heard and a very loud tone, he said, "Chef, what the #@*#~#@*^ is quiche?"

This was not going well. Others in the room looked to see what was going on, and some started to come over to my station. I thought to myself that this could be a quick end to my career, but I stood proud and said, "But sir, quiche is the newest omelet. It has a variety of fillings like cheese, bacon, ham, onions, and eggs all baked in a deep dish of pastry to make it a hearty meal. We designed the dish just for you guys. It is like an omelet pie."

He stood there a moment, and then said, "Let me try a piece." I gave him a slice, and he just about ate the whole thing in one bite. He then said in the same voice, "This quiche stuff is good, man. I'll take some more. The others clapped and lined up as he grabbed a whole quiche and said, "Thanks Chef, it is good, but change the damn name, will you?"

After the event was over, the client came and thanked us for the successful party. We just looked at each other and took away a few lessons. First, know your customer prior to planning and serving food. Second, ask more questions so you can better understand a function and its purpose before running off and planning it. And finally, think very fast on your feet and remember that real men do not eat quiche!

Oh the journey! Always a new road, always a new venture gained. Man, I love this chef stuff.

Quiche Lorraine My Way
(6–8 servings)

Ingredients

One 10-inch	Pie shell, baked halfway, with flat bottom
7 oz.	Crisp pancetta, diced
4 oz.	Onion, diced and sautéed
2 oz.	Tomato, diced
3 oz.	Mozzarella, shredded
1 oz.	Parmigiano-Reggiano cheese, grated
2	Eggs
2	Egg yolks
1 cup	Heavy cream
$1/2$ cup	Milk
1 tbsp.	Basil, minced
Pinch	Salt
Pinch	Pepper

Method

On bottom of pie shell, spread pancetta, onion, and tomato.
Sprinkle with both cheeses.
Make custard by mixing next 7 ingredients well.
Pour into pie shell.
Bake at 360° until the quiche is nice and brown and the custard just set, about 25–35 minutes.

Quiche Ariadna Style
(8 servings)

Ingredients

One 10-inch	Pie shell, baked halfway, with flat bottom
4 oz.	Apple-smoked bacon, cooked until crisp and diced (reserve fat)
8 oz.	Onions, sliced thin and sautéed in duck fat and the bacon fat
2 oz.	Porcini mushrooms, sliced and sautéed in duck fat
1	Potato, cooked and diced
3 oz.	Imported Gruyère cheese, shredded
1 tbsp.	Truffle, sliced or chopped
2	Eggs
2	Egg yolks
1 cup	Heavy cream
1/2 cup	Milk
2 tsp.	Truffle oil
Pinch	Salt
Pinch	Pepper

Method

On bottom of pie shell, spread out bacon, onions, mushrooms, potato, and truffles.

Sprinkle with Gruyère.

Make custard by mixing next 7 ingredients well; pour into pie shell.

Bake at 360° until quiche is nice and brown and the custard just set, about 25–35 minutes.

Cosette's Breakfast Quiche
(6–8 servings)

Ingredients

1/2 cup	Roasted pepper, chopped
1/2 cup	Onions, diced
1 clove	Garlic, minced
1/2 cup	Tomatoes, diced
8 oz. package	Chopped spinach, defrosted
1/2 cup	Cremini mushrooms, sliced
1/2 lb.	Pancetta bacon, diced
8	Eggs
3 tbsp.	Extra virgin olive oil
1 cup	Half & half
1/2 cup	Provolone cheese, shredded
1/2 cup	Mozzarella cheese, shredded
1 tsp.	Salt
1/2 tsp.	Crushed red pepper
1 tsp.	Basil
1/2 tsp.	Oregano
1	10-inch pie shell

Method

Sauté peppers, onions, garlic, tomatoes, and mushrooms until tender.
Bake pie shell at 375° for 5 minutes (use pie weights or beans to keep crust down).
Break eggs and mix in bowl. Stir in half & half, olive oil, salt, and crushed red pepper.
Add remaining ingredients and mix thoroughly.
Pour mixture into pie shell. Place pie shell on baking sheet to prevent spilling.
Bake at 350° for about 45 minutes or until tester comes out clean. Let sit for 5 minutes before serving.

Grilled Pizza Margarita
(6 individual pizzas)

Pizza Dough

Ingredients

1¹/₂ cups	Warm water
2¹/₂ tsp. (1 envelope)	Dried yeast
1 tbsp.	Molasses
2 tsp.	Kosher salt
2 tbsp.	Extra virgin olive oil
3–4 tbsp.	Oil for oiling and stretching dough
3¹/₂ cups	Unbleached white all-purpose flour
¹/₂ cup	Whole wheat flour

Method

Place the water, yeast, and molasses in the bowl of a mixer and let stand until slightly foamy, 10 minutes.

Add the salt and 2 tbsp. oil and mix with the dough hook on low speed.

Add the flours and mix on low speed to obtain a smooth dough that pulls away from the side of the mixer, 8 to 10 minutes. If dough is too wet, add a little more flour.

Note: The dough can also be made in a food processor. In this case, add the dry ingredients first, then the wet ingredients.

Divide the dough into 6 balls.

Arrange on a lightly oiled baking sheet and brush each ball with a little oil.

Cover the dough balls with plastic wrap.

Let the dough rise at room temperature until soft and puffy, 30–60 minutes.

Punch down and let the dough rise again.

Sauce

Ingredients

2 cups (1 28-oz. can)	Plum tomatoes, canned, drained
¹/₄ cup	Extra virgin olive oil
¹/₂ cup	Fresh basil, chopped
1¹/₂ tbsp.	Fresh garlic, minced
To taste	Salt and freshly ground black pepper

Method

While dough is rising, purée the tomatoes in the food processor.
Grind in the oil, basil, garlic, and salt and pepper to taste and set aside.
Note: This may make a little more sauce than you need. Serve any excess
with pasta.

Assembly and Grilling

Ingredients

3 cups (about 5 oz.)	Fontina and Pecorino Romano cheese, mixed, grated
3 tbsp.	Flat leaf parsley, finely chopped
6 tbsp.	Extra virgin olive oil

Method

Place the cheeses in a bowl, and gently toss to mix. Have ready the
parsley and olive oil, the former in a bowl, the latter in a cruet or
measuring cup.
Set up your grill for direct grilling and preheat to high, leaving one section
of your grill on medium. (This is also known as building a 2-zone fire.)
Working on an oiled baking sheet or pastry marble, stretch out the dough
balls to form very thin 12-inch ovals. Brush and oil the grill grate.
Gently lift a dough circle, taking care not to tear it, and drape it on the
grill grate over the hot part of the fire. The dough should start to rise and
blister immediately. Grill until the bottom is golden brown all over, about
2 minutes. (Lift the edge of the dough with a spatula to check it.)
Invert the dough circle and move it to the cooler part of the grill. Lightly
brush the top with olive oil and sprinkle with 1/2 cup of the mixed
cheeses. (The cheese should go all the way to the edge.) Place 8 or 10
dollops of tomato sauce (about 1 tbsp. each) on top of the pizza in
random spots. Sprinkle with 1/2 tbsp. chopped parsley and drizzle with
1 tbsp. oil.
Gently slide the pizza to the edge of the hot section of the grill. Grill until
the bottom is golden brown, rotating the pizza to cook the crust evenly.
Cook until the cheese is melted and the bottom of the crust is golden
brown. (You may need to move the pizza directly over the hot part of the
grill for a minute to finish the crust.)
Serve at once.
Assemble the remaining pizzas the same way.

Mark Ammerman 2004

Chef-Wheel Drive

*I*n Farmington, Connecticut, they hold an annual horse show at the fairgrounds. It is a big event with riders from all over competing for prizes and ribbons. I was not knowledgeable about these types of shows or about horses, except for a good recipe or two. (Only kidding about the recipes.)

My company was contracted to cater the event one year and to make sure that the food would be something special. It is times like these that a corporate chef gets called in and handed the responsibility for producing a successful event. I had to plan the whole week from start to finish, making the arrangements for chefs and cooks to come in and stay at the closest hotel, arranging service staff, ordering, and, more important, drawing up kitchen shift schedules.

Large events—especially at fairgrounds, people's houses, and other such venues—usually do not have proper kitchens available to produce the food that is needed. Depending on the size of a function, portable kitchens may be brought in. Tents with floors can be set up and all kinds of equipment put in place that run on electric or butane gas. This event would be no different; the kitchen and snack bar facilities were small, and they would not meet the health code regulations for such an operation. Luckily, we had a property not too far away with a good-sized kitchen we could use for basic prep and cooking.

The menus consisted of basic food items. We would serve breakfast, lunch, and dinner and cater for groups in the corporate tents. Companies paid big money for these and would entertain their clients with a good spot to sit and view the show. Egg sandwiches, pancakes, burgers, sandwiches, signature sandwiches, soups, desserts, and an array of gourmet platters would serve a wide spectrum of people from the riders, to horse trainers, volunteers, workers, staff, guests, and the corporate elite of the tent area. It would be a week of big-time food production that had to be of the highest quality regardless of the challenges we had with the venue.

I learned quickly in life that the more you accomplish the more people expect of you. The client for the show heard about my competitions and many awards and the awards the other chefs in the company had won for their cookery on my culinary team. This was one of the reasons we got the job. They even put an article in the newspaper with an interview titled "This Chef Is Not Horsing Around When It Comes to Food." As if that was not bad enough, they insisted on including a picture of me with seven gold medals around my neck. Not only were expectations going to be high from the client and the company for this event, but now the people attending the show would expect this great new food!

During my apprentice years, there was a learning curve that allowed you to make mistakes, and even though you might get in trouble with Chef and pay the price, it was expected. Expectations of you and your cooking were at an entry level, and at the end of the day the chef was the one responsible and would take the heat or the credit. You were just part of the team. Once the title of master chef is earned, however, and the more accolades you receive, the more people expect. Become a master chef and let me tell you, my friend, magic better be made in your kitchen!

Pressure and expectations are part of the rush and part of the territory. It is amusing to see these famous athletes whine during the first year or two that the fans and the organization expect so much. Well, if you take the cash, fame, and benefits, you'd better produce, plain and simple. Likewise, if you want to be a top chef with the title and accomplishments under your belt, then you have to produce and live up to the reputation.

Well, the week of the event started. I put each of my best chefs in charge of a specific location. The real nice stuff and corporate tents, believe it or not, were the easy part of this whole gig. Cooking and producing fine food with a talented crew is not hard; it's the fun part of the job. The real challenge comes in making an area such as a snack bar serve up a great burger, sandwich, or salad and doing it fast. How could a simple burger or hot dog excite people? By making them the best they can be and using quality products such as a good chopped meat for hamburger and quality buns and condiments.

Making the simple foods very good and serving them fast so people do not wait long is the hardest thing to do. Although people want quality, they want it fast in those situations, and if it is not good, you will hear about it. It is amazing that someone would think that a good-quality hamburger should only take 30 seconds to cook.

The first few days went well; the crowds would not really start until the weekend, so the first part of the week would be spent climbing the learning curve. My main job was to be everywhere at all times and ensure that all was running smoothly, from the service to the quality and timeliness of the food. I also was to visit the high-profile areas, corporate tents, organizer areas, and so on. All my lead chefs had two-way radios (there were no cell phones back then). We also had golf carts for transporting food products and getting to the various areas, and I had a four-wheel-drive dune buggy to get around quickly.

Business really started to pick up as the week went on. One of the simplest items we prepared was a 12-inch fruit kabob with fresh fruit and cheese. These turned out to be very popular, and we needed a refrigerator truck by the week's end with three prep cooks in it cutting, marinating, and skewering fruit.

Breakfast was big as well, especially with the trainers and workers at the show. There is a true art to breakfast cookery. One day, we got so busy I decided to jump in on the grill and help. Not a good idea. I learned that remembering 10 sandwiches and breakfast orders at one time and cooking them quickly was a bit different from fine dining. I sent out the wrong items—eggs with bacon instead of sausage, eggs with cheese, or was that no cheese? The grill cooks were getting a bit angry. When the scrambled egg mix hit my flying spatula and a quart of eggs went all over the grill, it was time to respect the wishes of the grill cooks and leave. If I came back to help, they would leave. "You may be the chef, but we are the grill cooks," they said.

So, after the egg disaster I went to make my rounds. We had a big catering job that day, and the corporate tents would be really busy. I received a call on the radio to bring some fruit and vegetables to the tent kitchen for the catering. I quickly hopped on my vehicle, loaded up, and was on my way. I loved cruising the show and would rev up the buggy for top speed.

I was flying toward the tent and decided to turn the accelerator handle a bit more, waving to the staff as I went by. Unfortunately, I turned the handle a bit too much. The buggy went up in the front in a wheelie; it kept going up, and I went with it! Then I went up in the air, as did the fruit and vegetables, and landed flat on my back. The buggy bounced around, and there I was in my chef coat and hat, fruit and vegetables all over me and a crowd of people gathering around. "Chef, Chef, you all right?" they asked.

I was embarrassed. The show's client came running when she heard what happened. The paramedics came and told me not to move. I kept arguing that I was fine and tried to get up. I was very sore, but my ego was bruised and I was embarrassed more than anything else.

The next morning I went to get my buggy (to drive carefully) and go over to the corporate tent for a meeting and to check the breakfast food. When I arrived, I found a large sign where the buggy was parked. It said: Reserved: The Chef's Horse Show Catering Vehicle Featuring CHEF-WHEEL DRIVE.

My chefs had a sense of humor and I had a sore butt.

Fruit Kabobs My Way
(12 servings)

Ingredients

12	Sugar cane skewers
1 cup	Water
1 cup	Sugar
2	Vanilla beans, split open
1 stick	Cinnamon
24	Strawberries, cleaned and stems removed
12 large	Cantaloupe balls
12 large	Honeydew melon balls
12 large	Watermelon balls
3	Peaches, quartered (12 quarters)

Method

Place water in stainless steel saucepan with sugar, vanilla, and cinnamon stick.

Bring to a boil and let simmer for 15 minutes, then remove from heat.

Start placing the fruit on the skewers, with one strawberry first, then the other four fruits, finishing with another strawberry.

Lay on a tray and brush the syrup mixture generously on each side of the fruit.

Let sit 5 minutes and serve.

My Breakfast Sandwich
(2 servings)

Ingredients

2	Bagels, halved and toasted
8 oz.	Corned beef hash, cooked
4	Eggs, poached
4 oz.	Light cheese sauce or hollandaise
1 tbsp.	Black olives, pitted and sliced
1 tsp.	Fresh parsley, chopped

Method

Arrange both bagel halves on a serving plate.
Spoon hash on both halves.
Top each half with a poached egg.
Spoon cheese or hollandaise sauce over egg.
Sprinkle with olives and parsley.

Salmon Club Sandwich
(6 servings)

Ingredients

12 (2$^1/_2$ oz.) slices	Fresh salmon
3 tbsp.	Olive oil
To taste	Kosher salt
To taste	Pepper
2	Avocados, sliced thin
2	Papayas, cleaned and sliced
18 slices	Smoked bacon, cooked
4	Endives, thinly cut
1	Cucumber, peeled, seeded, and sliced thin
2 tbsp.	Extra virgin olive oil
3	Shallots, minced
4 oz.	Honey
6 oz.	BBQ sauce
18 slices	White bread, toasted

Method

Season salmon with salt and pepper and olive oil.

Pan sear 1–2 minutes on each side. Salmon should have a nice brown color and be firm. Let cool.

Toss cucumber slices with extra virgin olive oil and season with salt and pepper.

Mix shallots, honey, BBQ sauce, and mayonnaise.

Pour 1 oz. of mixture into cucumbers and mix.

Lay out slices of toasted bread, and spread the remaining sauce on them. Equally distribute the cucumber slices among the bread slices.

On 6 slices, place endive with 1$^1/_2$ slices of bacon.

On 6 more slices, place the slices of salmon.

On the remaining 6 slices of bread, place the papaya, avocado, and the remaining bacon. Stack the bread slices club sandwich style, fasten with sandwich picks, cut in fours, and serve with homemade vegetable chips or potato chips.

Egg and Bacon Puff
(8 servings)

Ingredients

14	Eggs
1½ cups	Heavy cream
8 slices	Bacon, cooked and chopped
3	Plum tomatoes, seeded and diced
4 oz.	Butter, melted
½ tsp.	Nutmeg
To taste	Salt and pepper
1 cup	Gruyère cheese, shredded
½ cup	Dried bread crumbs
8	Cream puff shells

Method

Mix eggs with cream, bacon, tomatoes, butter, nutmeg, and salt and pepper.

Fold in ¾ of the cheese.

Line 8 ramekin molds with some pan spray, then coat with some breadcrumbs. Reserve remaining crumbs.

Place ramekins in 2-inch hotel pan with an inch of warm water.

Fill ramekins with egg mixture.

Top with remaining cheese and crumbs.

Bake in 350° oven until just firm in center, about 6–8 minutes, depending on your oven.

Let sit in oven with door open 2–3 minutes.

Cut 8 medium cream puff shells in half horizontally, take baked eggs out of ramekins and place in bottom halves of puffs, then place top halves over eggs and serve.

Steak Sandwich
(6 servings)

Ingredients

6 (8 oz. each)	Prime rib-eye steaks
1 oz.	Olive Oil
1 tsp.	Kosher salt
1 cup	Worcestershire sauce
4 tbsp.	Dijon mustard
6 oz.	Mayonnaise
2 tbsp.	Extra virgin olive oil
2 tsp.	Steak seasoning
1 tsp.	Granulated garlic
30	Onion rings, thinly sliced, breaded, and fried
6	French rolls, toasted, open face

Method

Mix olive oil, salt, Worcestershire sauce, and mustard thoroughly.

Pour over steaks and let marinate for at least 1 hour.

While the steaks are marinating, mix mayonnaise, extra virgin olive oil, steak seasoning, and granulated garlic thoroughly.

Grill steaks to your preferred degree of doneness.

Serve on an open-face French roll that's been toasted.

Top with mayonnaise mixture and fried onions.

Reader's Notes and Thoughts

Tailgating the Chef's Way

One of my duties as corporate chef was to entertain important clients or guests from overseas from time to time. This could be done over a nice lunch, dinner at a great restaurant, or at a theatre or sporting event. One year we secured tickets to a few New York Giants and New York Jets football games.

I was to be in charge of all tailgating preparations. Company chefs, executives, and clients would gather about 2 hours before game time and we would tailgate—eat, drink, talk, play cards, and generally enjoy the fun-filled atmosphere. Hot dogs, burgers, salads, and such were a big part of the event, along with beer, soft drinks, and nice wine, if the clients we had with us enjoyed such.

For one game, we had four very important clients and some executives from London attending. I decided it was time to take tailgating up a notch by preparing some very cool and delicious food that was not usually found at a football game. The menu consisted of the following tasty items: coconut shrimp with ginger sesame sauce, truffles, swordfish, Buffalo Chili, Kitchen Table Brownies and other items such as venison loins, pork chops, burgers, hot dogs, and sausages.

I went all out and even had a small stove that was hooked up to butane gas. I also took a stainless steel table from our catering kitchen and three grills.

The people from my company and the clients arrived in a deluxe van full of beverages, two TV sets, and, of course, a card table. We went to town cooking with all the grills going full tilt and the stove burners filled with food. The whole scene stood out even for a tailgate event. Some people started to come over after seeing this display of cooking and the buffet. They were even offering to buy some of the unique items we were cooking. We could have opened up shop and probably made some good money!

Some of the bigger groups who were also cooking came by to exchange food, and I met another working chef who was there cooking with his family.

Before you knew it, the parking lot looked like a neighborhood block party! Everyone was there to see the football game, but the conversation and friendships started over a thing called food.

These tailgate chefs talked about their recipes—the famous winning chili recipe; the chocolate cake recipe; and cookie, brownie, and sausage recipes. This was not a place to display an ego or see who could cook better than whom. That day in that stadium parking lot, every one cooking was a chef. They all were people with a passion for cooking and for providing hearty food and drink before the big game for friends and guests. People from different walks of life, different jobs, and different income levels were all having a great time, brought together by food and the love of a sport. The power of food and the power of cooking together is a great thing.

Coconut Shrimp with Ginger Dipping Sauce
(4 servings)

Coconut Shrimp

Ingredients

1¹/₂ lbs.	Large shrimp, peeled and deveined, tails intact
3	Large eggs
2 tbsp.	Water
1 tbsp.	Lime juice
1 tbsp.	Tabasco sauce or other hot pepper sauce
To taste	Salt
3 cups	Unflavored bread crumbs
1 cup	All purpose flour
2 cups	Shredded sweet coconut
1 tsp.	Cayenne pepper
6 cups (approximately)	Vegetable oil

Method

Wash shrimp and pat dry.
Whisk together eggs, water, lime juice, hot pepper sauce, and salt.
Line a baking sheet with waxed paper.
Combine bread crumbs, flour, coconut, and cayenne.
Hold on to shrimp by the tail and dip into egg mixture.
Roll shrimp in coconut mixture and place on the lined baking sheet.
Cover lightly and refrigerate 1 hour.
Deep fry until golden brown.

Ginger Dipping Sauce
(2 cups)

Ingredients

1 cup	Light soy sauce
¹/₂ cup	Orange marmalade
¹/₄ cup	Fresh ginger, minced
¹/₂ cup	Rice wine vinegar

Method

Combine all ingredients in small saucepan over medium heat.
Bring to a boil and immediately remove from heat; let rest 30 minutes.
Strain into serving bowl and serve at room temperature.

High-Energy Truffles
(Approximately 32 truffles)

Ingredients

1/2 cup	Walnuts or pecans, chopped
1/2 cup	Honey
1 tbsp.	Flour
1/2 cup	Peanut butter, chunky style
1 cup	Granola or all natural cereal
1 tbsp.	Vanilla
1 tbsp.	Wheat germ
	Semisweet chocolate, melted
	White chocolate, melted

Method

Mix and blend all ingredients (except melted chocolates) thoroughly until everything is well incorporated. If mixture is still a little grainy, fruit juice may be added.

Roll small pieces of mixture into balls approximately 1/2 oz. in weight.

Coat by dipping half the truffles into semisweet chocolate and the remaining half in white chocolate.

Allow to set.

Pipe opposite color chocolate on each truffle to create a decorative pattern.

Tailgate Grilled Swordfish
(8 servings)

Ingredients

8 tbsp.	Butter, cut into $1/2$-inch pieces
1 tbsp.	Fresh lemon juice, strained
1 tbsp.	Tarragon leaves, finely cut, or $1/2$ tsp. crumpled dried tarragon
2 lbs.	Swordfish steak, cut $1^1/2$ inches thick—a total of 8 pieces
1 tsp.	Salt
To taste	Black pepper
1 tbsp.	Vegetable oil
2	Lemons, cut into wedges

Method

Light a layer of briquettes in charcoal broiler, burning until white ash appears, or preheat range broiler at highest setting.

Melt butter; do not allow to brown.

Remove from heat and add lemon juice and tarragon.

Sprinkle swordfish steaks with salt and pepper.

Spread oil over hot grill or broiler and place the swordfish on it; brush top with 2 tbsp. of melted butter mixture.

Broil 3–4 inches from heat, basting with remaining butter.

Cook swordfish about 8 minutes each side or until it is evenly and delicately browned and firm to the touch.

Serve with lemon wedges.

New York Jets Buffalo Chili
(2 quarts)

Ingredients

3 lbs.	Top round or sirloin of Buffalo cut into 1/4-inch cubes
6 tbsp.	Grapeseed oil
2 cups	Onion, diced
4 cloves	Garlic, sliced thin
4 tbsp.	Ariadna's Chili Spice
1 tsp.	Oregano
1 tsp.	Ground cumin
1 tsp.	Red pepper flakes
1 6-oz. can	Tomato paste
1 cup	Tomatoes, diced
3 cups	Beef broth
1 tsp.	Salt
To taste	Freshly ground black pepper
1 1/2 cups	Red kidney beans, freshly cooked, or canned kidney beans, drained

Method

Pat meat dry with paper towel.

In a heavy skillet, cook meat in 4 tbsp. oil over high heat for 2–3 minutes until lightly browned. Remove meat, leaving oil and juices in skillet. Reserve meat.

Add 2 tbsp. oil to skillet and cook onion and garlic 4–5 minutes.

Remove skillet from heat and add chili powder, oregano, cumin, and pepper flakes; stir.

Add tomato paste, tomatoes, beef stock, salt, and a few grindings of black pepper.

Combine this with the meat in a pot and simmer with pot half covered for 1 1/2 hours or until meat is tender.

Add beans 15 minutes before meat is done.

Kitchen Table Brownies
(12 servings)

Brownies

Ingredients

¹/₂ cup	Unsalted butter
12 oz.	Semisweet chocolate, broken into pieces
1 cup	Granulated sugar
4	Eggs
4 tbsp.	Hot water, 120°–130°
2 tsp.	Pure vanilla extract
1¹/₂ cups	Flour
¹/₂ tsp.	Baking soda
Pinch	Salt

Method

Preheat oven to 350°. Grease half sheet pan lightly and line base with parchment paper.

In a medium saucepan, combine butter and chocolate pieces over extremely low heat, stirring constantly, until melted and smooth.

Stir in sugar, eggs, water, and vanilla until combined.

Add flour, baking soda, and salt, stirring well.

Spread half of the chocolate mixture in pan using a hot palette knife.

Top this with a layer of the cream cheese filling, spreading as evenly as possible.

Spread the remaining brownie mixture as evenly as possible over cream cheese filling.

Swirl the top pan mixture using a knife to give the batter an evenly distributed marble effect.

Bake for 25–30 minutes. DO NOT OVERBAKE. Brownies should be moist in center.

When cool, cut brownies into squares.

Cream Cheese Filling

Ingredients

16 oz.	Cream cheese, room temperature
1 cup	Sugar
2	Eggs
2 tsp.	Pure vanilla extract

Method

Combine ingredients and beat until smooth.

Flambé Away

Being a chef gives you the opportunity to create things that you hope will impress the guest. Special functions or parties that are out of the norm can be fun because you get a chance to be more creative and, in some cases, depending on the client, a chance to go all out. Every chef loves a big-money event for which the client wants the best of everything and cost is no object.

In the beginning of my career as a chef, I ran a catering department for a company called Culinary Table. We catered for everything from airlines to hotels, corporate dining rooms, and commercial cafeterias. At one point, we received a contract for a function called The Fish Harvest. It was an event for a very prominent company that would be entertaining its most important customers. Food for the 4-day event would be served on a boat. (Oh, the memories from my apprenticeship!) Breakfast, lunch, a themed party, and an upscale BBQ would be held at a mansion in Greenwich, Connecticut.

This was a chance to show our stuff. The contract was worded so that if we gave a great performance the first year, we would automatically receive the contract for the next 3 years. Our bid to win the contract took a lot of effort, and we competed against a very well-known catering house in Westchester, New York, and a premier catering house in New York City. It was now time to walk the walk after all of our sales talk.

I needed the best chefs I had and a support team who would work endless hours and rise to the occasion. The event was so time consuming that we actually had to book rooms at a nearby hotel for those of us who would be working on only 4 to 5 hours sleep every night.

The front-of-the-house staff spent endless hours planning the event. The merchandising department had to come up with the theme and decorate all the events, and the culinary department had to come up with all the menus. The menu planning was tedious; this had to be the crème de la crème. The menus took more than 2 weeks of research and writing for a total of 16 meals. They all had to be of the highest quality; even breakfast had to be something special, with items such as fresh-made blintzes, poached eggs with fresh crabmeat and a tomato hollandaise, and fresh-baked pastries. We even had fresh-squeezed juice.

The themed event was a formal affair—a night in Paris. All the décor, dress, and menus reflected this theme; the guests dressed in formal attire that had a French look and in French designer clothes, and the room was turned into a French-style theatre for an after-dinner show.

The dinner was a classical menu featuring four courses and a grand finale, which was a tableside flambé of Crêpes Suzette and Baked Alaska Grand Surprise. We started the meal with a flavorful consommé of chicken, followed by a superb fish course of fresh Dover sole filled with a delicate shrimp mousse and scallops finished with Sauce American. The main plate was roasted beef Wellington, sauce Bordelaise, cauliflower gratin, and glazed carrots. The fourth course was a simple but flavorful salad of greens, roasted tomato sorbet, and baked Brie.

The work for the meal was tremendous. We prepared day and night, boning fish, making stocks, and ensuring that only the finest ingredients came through the door from our suppliers. The chefs and cooks gave me everything they had, and most important, they worked as a team.

The meal was served, and course after course was received with applause and great reviews from the guests. Then it was time for dessert. We started setting up the three carts to wheel into the dining room for a spectacular display of flambé. We checked to be sure all items were on the carts: copper pans, liquor, crêpes, cherries, ice cream, and the baked Alaskas. We positioned all the carts in the dining rooms, and the chefs lined up for service.

The object was for all three chefs to start their desserts at the same time. Then, the lights would go out and they would flambé away.

Well, we started to cook, the lights went dim, and there we were—flaming away except for one cart. The guests gave "ohs" and "ahhs," but one cart was not in flame at all. I quickly went over to see what was wrong. The chef was not getting the liquor near enough to the flame to light and give the guests a show.

I jumped in, hastily pushing him aside and mumbling (so the guests did not to hear me) that I was displeased with him and not happy that the finale was not perfect.

I turned up the flame and held the bottle high, pouring the brandy that would flame the sauce for the crêpes. The flame caught, as did the stream of brandy flowing from the bottle. I did not notice this as I set the bottle down. The other chef was so nervous by now that he hit the bottle as I placed it on the table, and the flaming brandy spilled onto the table.

I took the sauce and poured it over plates of crêpes and ice cream while the area next to me was on fire. The chef's apron caught on fire as he tried to put out the flames on the tablecloth. Then he hit the table, spilling Sterno across the table as well. So, there I was with a huge fire of brandy and Sterno in front of me.

The guests were applauding and did not really see what was going on, thinking "Wow, what a flambé!" Little did they know how serious it was; they thought it was part of the show!

The chef went running in the back with his apron on fire; the table fire was dying out as I covered it with the ice cream bucket and ice, not missing a beat with the service. The flames died out in the pan as we served the last portions of crêpes. When the lights went on, the guests all stood and applauded the whole team for such a great dinner and display of flambé.

Over all, the event was a success and we received the contract for the next 3 years, but the party planner in charge of the function did notice the flambé event and suggested that we plan something a bit safer for the future events.

That night I learned that reacting too fast and making others too nervous was not a good way to train and ensure success in the long term. What might have been a serious incident could have been prevented by taking a slower course of action.

Even though I share the memories of such events with my chefs and get a big laugh, they are always there to teach you for the future.

Cosette's Creamy New York Cheesecake
(two 8-inch cheesecakes)

Ingredients

3 cups	High-quality cream cheese
1²/₃ cups	Sugar
4 large	Eggs
1 tbsp.	Pure vanilla
1 pod	Vanilla bean, scraped
¹/₃ tsp.	Salt
4 cups	Fresh sour cream

Method

Cream sugar and cream cheese in a mixer until smooth.

Add eggs, one at a time.

Add all remaining ingredients and mix for 2–3 minutes more.

Line two 8-inch springform pans with graham cracker crust.

Divide the filling into the two pans.

Bake in water bath at 350° for 25–40 minutes, or until the mixture sets in the middle.

Let cool.

Serve with fresh strawberries and sauce and fresh whipped cream.

Chef Ed's Bananas Foster
(4 servings)

Spice Butter

Ingredients

8 tbsp. (1 stick)	Salted butter
3 tbsp.	Brown sugar
3 tbsp.	Dark rum
1 tsp.	Ground cinnamon
1/2 tsp.	Ground allspice
1/8 tsp.	Ground cloves
4 large	Bananas
4 scoops	French vanilla ice cream

For flambéing (optional)

4 tbsp.	Rum, dark or 151 proof

Method

To prepare the spice butter, melt the butter in a saucepan.
Add the sugar, rum, and spices and bring to a boil over medium high heat.
Boil the mixture until syrupy, 2–4 minutes.
Remove the pan from the heat and set aside.

Cut each banana in half lengthwise, and brush the cut sides with spice butter.
Arrange the bananas in a sauté pan, cut side down, and sauté until nicely browned, about 4 minutes.
Turn the bananas over and sauté for another 2–3 minutes.
Keep basting the bananas with more spice butter. Transfer the bananas to a platter or plates and drizzle with the remaining spice butter.
Top with ice cream.

To flambé the bananas, warm the 4 tbsp. rum in a small saucepan. Do not let it get hot or boil. With sleeves rolled up, hair tied back, and face averted, tip the pan toward the flames or touch a match to it to set the rum afire.
Pour the flaming rum over the bananas and serve at once.

Kahlúa Cake
(one 9-inch cake)

Crust

Ingredients

¹/₂ cup	Graham cracker crumbs
¹/₂ cup	Walnuts, finely chopped
1 cup	Almonds, finely chopped
¹/₂ cup	Sugar
1 stick (¹/₂ cup)	Unsalted butter, melted

Method

Preheat oven to 350°. Lightly oil a 9¹/₂ × 2 inch springform pan.
In a bowl, stir together crust ingredients until combined well, and press onto bottom of pan.
Bake crust in middle of oven 15 minutes, or until pale golden color, and cool in pan on a rack.

Chocolate Layer

Ingredients

2 cups	Heavy cream
16 oz.	Semisweet chocolate, coarsely chopped
2 tbsp.	Light corn syrup
1 stick (¹/₂ cup)	Unsalted butter, cut into pieces

Method

In a saucepan heat cream, chocolate, and corn syrup over moderately high heat, stirring occasionally, until chocolate is melted and mixture just comes to a boil.
Remove pan from heat and stir in butter, one piece at a time, until smooth.
Pour mixture over crust in pan and chill until firm, about 3 hours.

Butter Cream Layer

Ingredients

1½ cups	Sugar
½ cup	Water
6 large	Egg yolks
3 sticks (1½ cups)	Unsalted butter, softened
½ cup	Kahlúa
4 oz.	Semisweet chocolate, chopped, melted, and cooled

Method

In a saucepan, cook sugar and water over moderately high heat, stirring occasionally, until sugar is melted.

Simmer syrup, undisturbed, until a candy thermometer registers 240°.

In a bowl, beat yolks with an electric mixer until smooth.

Add hot syrup in a stream, beating on high speed until thickened and cooled.

Reduce speed to medium and beat in butter, a little at a time.

Beat in Kahlúa and chocolate until combined well.

Assembly

Spread butter cream over chocolate layer and chill until firm, about 3 hours.

Run a knife around edge of pan and carefully remove side of pan.

Baked Pumpkin Mousse with Ginger Cream
(8 servings)

Pumpkin Mousse

Ingredients

1¹/₂ cups	Light cream
¹/₈ tsp.	Salt
1 tsp.	Cinnamon
1¹/₄ tsp.	Ginger, powdered
Generous pinch	Allspice
Generous pinch	Cloves, powdered
Generous pinch	Nutmeg
2 tbsp.	Dark Rum
3	Eggs
¹/₂ cup	Sugar
1 cup	Canned solid-pack pumpkin (not pie filling)
	Finely grated rind of 1 orange

Method

Preheat oven to 325°, and place rack in center of oven.
Bring cream to a slight boil on medium heat.
In a cup, mix salt, cinnamon, ginger, allspice, cloves, nutmeg, and rum.
Mix eggs slightly; add spices and rum, then pumpkin and orange rind and mix until smooth.
Add a little of the cream mixing well, then add remaining cream mix until smooth.
Place mixture evenly in eight 4-oz. buttered cups.
Place in a shallow pan and fill halfway with hot water while in the oven.
Cover with a sheet pan or foil, and bake 40–45 minutes until firm.
Garnish with Ginger Cream.

Ginger Cream

Ingredients

1 cup	Heavy cream
2 tbsp.	Confectioners sugar
1/2 tsp.	Vanilla extract
2 tbsp.	Grand Marnier or Curaçao
2 tbsp.	Crystallized ginger, very finely cut, or preserved ginger, drained

Method

In a chilled bowl with chilled beaters, whip the cream, sugar, vanilla, and Grand Marnier or Curaçao only until the mixture holds a soft shape. Fold in the ginger.

Crème Brûlée
(8 servings)

Ingredients

4 cups	Heavy cream
8	Egg yolks
1/4 cup plus 1 tbsp.	Granulated sugar
2 tsp.	Vanilla extract
1 cup	Light brown sugar

Method

Heat oven to 325° and place rack in center of oven.

Sift brown sugar and dry on top of hot oven.

Bring cream to slight boil.

In a bowl, mix egg yolks until just beaten.

Add granulated sugar to cream and dissolve.

Add a few spoonfuls of cream at a time to egg yolks; stir lightly, DO NOT LET MIXTURE GET FOAMY.

Mix in vanilla.

Bake in individual or a shallow ovenproof dish placed in a shallow pan filled 1/2 way with hot water.

Let cool, top with sifted light brown sugar, and then brown with salamander or torch.

Reader's Notes and Thoughts

Coach to Chef

*B*eing a chef was not only living a dream; it was a chance to always find a day filled with new challenges and the excitement of preparing food in new and different ways. It also gave me the opportunity to train others and to help keep them from making the errors I made.

The job of chef is pressure filled, with the demand to perform at a high level nightly. It is similar to being in a performance on the theatre stage. The ability to cook and serve consistently great food takes a great deal of emotion and energy. Not everyone understands this. Even the people that work with you, such as the front-of-the-house managers, do not understand the emotional highs and lows and the mental preparation it takes to perform and strive to reach a level of perfection that in most cases will never be met. When I have a very important function or meal, the emotional and mental preparation is more tiring than the physical preparation.

There are also times that you are called upon to serve people of notoriety or fame, which is always fun. I had such an opportunity in 1994 when I worked at a restaurant in Greenwich, Connecticut, that I helped open and became the executive chef for. The restaurant at 64 Greenwich Avenue was a collaboration between myself and my friend Chef Brad Barnes. We served American contemporary cuisine. The restaurant had two floors that were smartly decorated, and it earned us three stars in our first year of operation before the big restaurant boom took over in Greenwich.

Our first celebrity guests were Kathy Lee Gifford and Regis Philbin; they used to frequent the restaurant quite often. We also had the honor of hosting Vanessa Williams and Stephanie Seymour, among others.

One night, while I was putting the finishing touches on the night's specials, the waiter came in and said, "Chef, you will never guess who sat down to eat."

"Who?" I wondered, as my crew and I worked feverishly to get ready for the evening's service.

"It is Pat Riley and his wife!"

The waiter knew I was a big New York Knicks fan, and Mr. Riley was the head coach at the time. Wow! This was really cool. I wondered if I should go and say hello or not. I did not want to be a pest to a person trying to dine peacefully with his wife. Also, the restaurant owners felt it was important to respect people's privacy when they came in to dine.

The Rileys were looking over the menu while the waiter was in the kitchen. He said, "They are most likely going to order just a salad and main plate." The order came in; it was a salad to split and two main plates.

Well, that night I had some awesome pencil white asparagus from Michigan and fresh blue crabmeat. I asked the pantry cook to hold off on the salad and went to work preparing a very special appetizer. I gently cooked the asparagus in butter, sautéed the crabmeat with some small diced vegetables, and added white wine and more butter. I laid the asparagus on the plates, gently spooned the crab and butter sauce over it, then finished the dish with roasted Meyer lemons.

The waiter brought out the starter as a selection from the chef for them to enjoy. After the plates came back, I went out briefly to say hello and ask whether they enjoyed the asparagus.

Coach introduced his wife and asked my name. He asked about the asparagus and the preparation of the dish and then asked me how many dinners I would serve that night. I answered around 180 to 220. He asked how many people were cooking, then he suggested that being a chef was like being a coach. Like a coach, I had to get my message across, and my cuisine and standards were accomplished through others.

I had never looked at it that way before. Regardless of the talent of a chef, his or her vision for the food, and the desire to exceed a customer's expectations, it had to be done through the cooks and staff in the kitchen. I could not cook all 200 meals alone.

I thanked the coach and said that it was a pleasure to meet him and went back to the kitchen for the night's business. About an hour later, the waiter showed up with a menu cover and said, "Here, Chef. This is for you." It was a our menu cover signed by Coach Riley, saying, "Best of luck, good cooking and the asparagus were great."

I was very pleased and inspired that evening. I even went out to purchase his book on teamwork, and I have used it as a guide to building and getting the most out of my culinary team.

That moment was one among the many in my career that I am grateful for and will always savor.

Coach's Crab Cakes and White Asparagus
(8 servings)

Crab Cakes

Ingredients

1	Shallot, diced fine
1 tbsp.	Butter
1 tsp.	Fresh thyme leaf, picked and minced
1	Egg
1/2 cup	Mayonnaise
2 tbsp.	Worcestershire sauce
1/2 tsp.	Cayenne pepper
1/2 tbsp.	Dry mustard
2 tsp.	Spice de Cosette seasoning
1/2 cup	Ritz crackers, ground, or bread crumbs made with brioche
2 lbs.	Lump crabmeat, shell free
As needed	Clarified butter or olive oil blend

Method

Sauté shallots lightly in 1 tbsp. butter until translucent and cool.

Combine all ingredients except crabmeat, using only 1/3 cup of crumbs, in bowl, and mix well.

Gently fold lump crabmeat into base. Shape into 4-oz. cakes, then coat with remaining crumbs.

Sauté cakes in clarified butter until golden brown.

Finish in 350° oven for 4–5 minutes.

Serve on a bed of white asparagus poached in butter.

Asparagus for Crab Cakes

Ingredients

24 oz.	White asparagus spears, pencil size
1 tsp.	Kosher salt
8 oz.	Butter
2/3 cup	Chicken broth
3 slices	Lemon

Method

Place butter, broth, and lemon slices in a stainless steel sauté pan with asparagus; sprinkle with salt.

Bring to a low simmer when butter melts; cook until tender.

Place on plate and spoon some of the broth over the asparagus.

Spring Fling Cobb Salad
(8 servings)

Ingredients

24 oz.	Romaine, chopped
6	Red endive, sliced
2	Avocadoes, diced
40	Raspberries
6 oz.	Goat cheese
1 lb.	Chicken breast, cooked and diced
16	Shrimp, grilled
8 slices	Pancetta, or bacon, cooked crisp
2 cups	Raspberry vinaigrette
1/2 cup	Almonds, toasted

Method

Toss romaine and endive with 4 oz. of vinaigrette and distribute in 8 bowls.

Garnish salad with the avocado, chicken, and goat cheese equally.

Place raspberries and shrimp on top.

Lace with vinaigrette, then top with almonds and a pancetta slice.

Note: Make sure the pancetta is crisp. Grill or broil the chicken breast for best flavor, but season lightly so as not to overpower the salad ingredients.

Cherry Balsamic Dressing
(2 cups)

Ingredients

3 oz.	Cherry syrup
1/4 cup	Extra virgin olive oil
1 cup	Grapeseed oil or blend
1/2 cup	Cherry balsamic vinegar
3 tbsp.	Anise honey
1 tsp.	Mint, chopped
2 tsp.	Basil, chopped
To taste	Salt and pepper

Method

Combine all ingredients in a blender and blend 1–2 minutes.

Chicken Sauté Chasseur with Parisian Potatoes
(4 servings)

Chicken Sauté Chasseur

Ingredients

1	3-lb. Chicken
1 cup	Flour
2 tbsp.	Kosher salt
1 tsp.	Black pepper
As needed	Clarified butter
2	Tomatoes, peeled, seeded, and diced
2	Shallots
6 oz.	Mushrooms
6 oz.	White wine
2 oz.	Butter
1 1/2 pints	Demi-glace
4 oz.	Brandy
1 tsp.	Tarragon, chopped
2 tsp.	Parsley, chopped
To taste	Salt and pepper

Method

Cut the chicken into 8 pieces.
Mix the flour with salt and pepper.
Dredge the chicken pieces with the flour.
Place enough clarified butter (about 2–3 oz.) in a sauté pan on high heat.
Place the chicken pieces in the pan.
Cook to golden brown on both sides (approximately 3–4 minutes).
Remove the chicken from the pan, discard excess fat, add chopped shallots to the butter, and sauté.
Add diced tomatoes and sliced mushrooms and cook for another 2 minutes.
Add white wine and reduce by half; simmer for 1 minute.
Add brandy carefully (it will flame).
Add demi-glace and tarragon, return the chicken to the sauce, and cook gently for 2–5 minutes.
Sprinkle with chopped parsley.

Parisian Potatoes
(4 servings)

Ingredients

1¹/₂ lbs.	Idaho potatoes
2 oz.	Butter
2 oz.	Oil
3 tbsp.	Parsley, chopped
To taste	Salt and white pepper

Method

Cut potatoes with a Parisian scoop (small melon ball cutter).
Heat oil and butter in heavy sauté pan.
Add potatoes and sauté until golden brown and soft.
Season and sprinkle with parsley.

BBQ Shanks of Veal Braciola Style
(6 servings)

Ingredients

Two, 2$\frac{1}{2}$–3 lbs. each	Veal shanks from milk-fed veal
4 cloves	Garlic, minced
3 tbsp.	Parsley, chopped
4 tbsp.	Pecorino Romano cheese, grated
$\frac{1}{2}$ tbsp.	Lemon rind, grated
To taste	Kosher salt
To taste	Black pepper
As needed	Olive oil
1	Onion, diced
2	Carrots, diced
3 cloves	Garlic, sliced
3 tbsp.	Tomato paste
$\frac{1}{2}$ cup	Red wine
1 cup	Demi-glace
1 pt.	Roma tomatoes, crushed
	Marrow bones from shank, whole or cut into 2-inch pieces

Method

Have the butcher bone the veal shanks for you, keeping the meat in one piece. Save the bones.

Flatten the meat with a mallet.

Combine garlic, parsley, cheese, and lemon rind.

Season shanks with salt and pepper.

Fill cavities of meat with the garlic mixture, roll, and tie with twine.

Put olive oil in brazier pot and brown meat well on both sides; reserve meat.

Add some more oil and sauté onions, garlic, and carrots.

When lightly brown, add tomato paste and cook well.

Deglaze pan with red wine.

Add veal broth and crushed tomatoes, stir, then add shank bones.

Place shanks on top and cover.

Braise in 350° oven until tender.

Remove shanks and bones.

Season sauce with salt and pepper, if needed.

Remove twine; slice shanks.

Serve with marrow from the shank bones, the sauce, soft polenta, and a warm slaw.

The Meal Must Go On

*M*y job at the Westchester Country Club is exciting. We serve a large variety of foods—everything from a simple hamburger (one of the best around) to classical French cuisine. We cover the gambit. During our prime season, we have numerous functions going all at once, and the team of 45 to 55 culinarians provides a wide array of food in many different locations. I remember many things about my first year at the club, but two days really stand out as being full of challenges and seeing people step up to the plate when needed.

One nice day in June, we had two functions in the main club, a big event at our beach club, and a full house at the restaurant. I was standing in the kitchen going over the day's events with my executive sous-chef and the rest of the team, when we heard a popping noise. Soon after that, all the lights went dead. We looked around and saw that the lights were out in every part of the club. Naturally, we rushed to check all stoves, ovens, refrigeration units, and such only to find that every single appliance was dead. No power, no stoves to cook on, nothing.

We waited a few minutes while security and engineering went to see what had happened. About 20 minutes later, we found out that a person working on the phone lines had drilled through the power line. This was a major power outage. Luckily, the person working on the phone lines survived and was not seriously hurt—that was the good news of the day. The bad news was that we had a pre-wedding party at 7:00 P.M., lunch would start in about 1 hour, and we had a big event at the beach club that day.

The easiest task to prepare for was the beach club function. It was about 5 to 6 miles off premise, so it was not affected by the happenings of the morning. The kitchens were not that large, but with some effort we could get the job done. My executive sous-chef got the team together and started loading the vans with all the prep and the food for this big event.

Meanwhile, the restaurant went into emergency mode, starting to get ready for a BBQ buffet. The power and kitchen equipment may have been out, but we could cook on gas grills! Out came the grills, and we were ready for lunch with no problem. The team worked quickly—everyone from the maintenance people who set up the tables and grills to engineering, housekeeping, and the front-of-the-house staff. Power or no power, our members would have a place to dine.

While things were progressing nicely, I received my next challenge: I found out the power was not expected to be back on until late that evening or the next day. It was still light out, and we had another 6 hours until dark. The restaurant had dinner hour to prepare for, and we still had the rehearsal dinner. We started working on the dinner first, trying to keep all refrigerator doors shut and using portable butane burners to cook. We were cooking veal, vegetables, and everything else on six portable burners and doing what was needed to have a great event. At the same time, the beach club event was going fine. Good news came when we found out that the restaurant would regain power by 5:00 P.M. at the latest.

So, two down and one to go. The grills came in handy again. We moved them to the terrace outside the function room to work on the food for the pre-wedding event. All went well, considering, and not a meal or function was missed. The power came back on around 9:00 P.M. just in time to save all the food we had in the refrigerated boxes.

You may think that is the end of my story, but it is not. Three months later, we had another power outage to deal with. Most people, especially those in the Northeast, remember the power grid outage in 2003 that caused most of the Northeast to be blacked out from Canada to the Midwestern United States. We were in the middle of getting ready for a demonstration bistro dinner at the time. It was to be a four-course meal featuring French bistro cuisine. I was to demonstrate each course the guests would be served, then I would go back into the kitchen to work with my team and serve the exact course the guests had just learned to cook.

The event was sold out, and the dining room was transformed into a stage like something you'd see on the Food Network. We worked very hard preparing for the event, and the first plate, a warm tomato tartin, took more than 3 days to prepare. It featured delicious tomatoes and goat cheese on a flaky, buttery puff pastry with pesto sauce.

The rest of the dinner took much effort as well. It included sea bass over a warm salad of spring vegetables, a main plate of filet mignon with a porcini mushroom crust, and a roasted pear with poppyseed lemon cake.

I was setting up the finishing touches for the stage while my culinary team looked over the final prep for the demos and the meal. Just then, "Boom!" All the lights and electricity went out. "Not again," I thought. "How could this happen twice in such a short time?" Perhaps this time it would be something minor and we would be back up and running in no time. Everyone had worked so hard on the set-up and promoting the event that I hoped we wouldn't have to reschedule it.

We set up candles and temporary lights in the kitchen so we could work. The banquet crew cleaned up a bit and got organized, although things did not look promising. Then we found out that this was a problem for the whole East Coast, from parts of Connecticut to New York City and even Ohio and Canada. People were speculating about what happened. Could it be a terrorist act? Did a person do this?

We had to make a call, though. It was getting late, and the guests for this sold-out event needed to know what was going on. An additional problem was that many people coming from New York might not be able to get home soon.

We cancelled the event. My poor tomato tartins! All the work for a night of fine cuisine on hold!

Meanwhile, we still had the restaurant issue to deal with. Many members lived in the apartments at the club. Those who were staying with us would need a place to eat. So, the grill and portable burners all came back out. Burgers, steaks, chicken, pasta, and a buffet of cold food would be ready for our members who needed something to eat.

The night turned out to be a huge success, with more than 300 members dining and having a great time by candlelight. The kitchen was aglow with candles, and the culinary team, as well as the other departments, pulled together to make it all happen. We fed the staff from the club who had worked so hard that night. Security, hotel and wait staff, and the maintenance and culinary crews all made it a fun-filled night for the members. (The bistro event happened the following week and was a huge success. And yes, we had to re-do the tomato tartins.)

I drove home that night in pitch dark, realizing how dark things can be without power and how we take this commodity for granted. When I got home, my family was huddled in a room around candles and flashlights eating snacks and drinking water. We talked, played, and laughed, and for one night the TV did not interfere or rule the house.

Did you know that America uses 50% of the world's resources? It would be great if everyone thought about that for a moment and about the lights we leave on that we do not need and the appliances that run constantly for no reason. Perhaps it will take a few more power outages to learn this lesson before it is too late. Power and resources, like food, should be respected and always handled with care and thoughtfulness.

Westchester Country Club
Tanqueray Cocktail Sauce
(1 quart)

Ingredients

1½ cups	Chili sauce
½ qt.	Heinz ketchup
	Juice of 3 lemons
2 tbsp.	Sugar
1 oz.	Frank's Red Hot sauce
1 oz.	French's Worcestershire sauce
½ cup	Prepared horseradish
4 oz.	Tanqueray gin
4 oz.	Red vermouth
½ cup	Cocktail olives, minced
½ cup	Parsley, finely chopped
¼ cup	Sage, finely chopped

Method

Mix all ingredients well and serve with favorite cold shellfish.

The Sports House Restaurant Foie Gras Grits
(8 servings)

Ingredients

2 cups	Quick-cooking grits
1 qt.	Chicken broth
½ qt.	Milk
1 tsp.	Kosher salt
2 oz.	Butter
10 oz.	Foie gras, diced

Method

Cook grits with broth, milk, salt, and butter.
Sautéed foie gras until nicely browned.
Fold into grits with fat from cooking.
Adjust seasoning with salt and pepper.

Creamy Red Wine Dressing
(2 cups)

Ingredients

1 cup	Heavy cream
1/2 cup	Mayonnaise
To taste	Kosher salt
1/3 cup	High-quality red wine
1/3 cup	Aged red wine vinegar
To taste	Pepper

Method

Whisk all ingredients together well.
Adjust seasoning.
This makes a great dressing for hearty greens, French beans, artichokes, and the like.

Chef Leonard's Gorgonzola Dressing
(4 cups)

Ingredients

1 clove	Garlic, minced
1/4 cup	Sweet onion, diced very small
2 tbsp.	Olive oil
1/4 cup	Pear vinegar
1 oz.	Red wine
1/2 oz.	Dry mustard
1 cup	Mayonnaise
1 cup	Pear vinegar
1 tbsp.	Hungarian paprika
2 tbsp.	Anise honey
1 tbsp.	Worcestershire sauce
To taste	White pepper
To taste	Kosher salt
2 cups	Grapeseed oil
1/2 cup	Extra virgin olive oil
8 oz.	Imported Gorgonzola cheese from Italy or another high-quality dolce style

Method

Sauté onion and garlic until very soft and light brown in 2 tbsp. olive oil.
Deglaze pan with 1/4 cup of pear vinegar; reserve.
Dissolve mustard in red wine.
Combine next 7 ingredients (mayonnaise–Kosher salt) and blend well in a blender.
Add oils slowly until well blended.
Add 6 oz. of cheese to dressing and blend with blender stick, then fold in the remaining 3 oz. by hand.

Tomato Tart Tartin
(8 servings)

Pistou Sauce

Ingredients

6–8 oz.	Fresh basil leaves
1 clove	Garlic, peeled
1 tsp.	Pine nuts, lightly toasted
2 tsp.	Parmesan cheese, grated
1/2 cup	Extra virgin olive oil

Method

Blanch basil leaves in boiling water.
Put all ingredients in food processor and process until smooth.

Tarts

Ingredients

10 large	Heirloom tomatoes, peeled, seeded, and cut in quarters
To taste	Salt and pepper
As needed	Extra virgin olive oil
8	Puff pastry circles, 4–6 inches
1	Egg wash made from 1 egg, 1 tsp. oil
1 tbsp.	Olive oil
1/2 oz.	Sweet butter
16 oz.	Onions, thinly sliced
1 tbsp.	Brown sugar
3 oz.	Red wine
1 tsp.	Tarragon, minced
To taste	Salt and pepper

Method

Layer tomato pieces into eight 3-inch round tart molds with removable bottoms.

Season with olive oil and salt and pepper.

Bake in 350° oven for 7–10 minutes, until tender. Reserve.

Preheat oven to 400°; place pastry circles on pan lined with parchment paper.

Refrigerate for 15–20 minutes until cold.

Poke holes in pastry with a fork.

Brush with egg wash and bake pastry until light brown. Reserve.

Heat 1 tbsp. olive oil and 1/2 oz. butter in pan.

Add onions and sauté until soft, about 5 minutes.

Add sugar and cook until onions are a nice brown color, about 10 minutes.

Deglaze pan with red wine; cook until almost evaporated.

Add tarragon and season; reserve.

Goat Cheese Mixture

Ingredients

1		Shallot, minced
2 tbsp.		Olive oil
6 oz.		Fresh goat cheese, room temperature
3 oz.		Fresh ricotta
2 tsp.		Heavy cream
3 tbsp.		Pistou sauce

Method

Sauté shallots until soft

Add all items and mix well.

Assembly

Take tart shells with tomatoes and divide goat cheese mixture among shells.

Divide onions over cheese.

Place pastry shell over each one. Place in 350° oven for 3–5 minutes.

Invert each pastry shell on the center of a plate.

Garnish with sauce and some mixed baby greens or frisée salad.

New England Shrimp Cobbler
(6 servings)

Sauce

Ingredients

1 qt.	Fish or shrimp stock
1/4 cup	Champagne vinegar
3 oz.	Sweet butter
3 oz.	Flour
1 oz.	Mushroom trimmings
1 oz.	Celery, diced
1 oz	Onion, diced
1 sprig	Thyme
2	Bay leaves
To taste	Salt and pepper
2–4 oz.	Heavy cream

Method

Bring stock to a boil. Add thyme, bay leaves, and vinegar; simmer.
Sauté vegetables in butter 3–5 minutes. Add flour, mix well, and cook
gently until roux turns light brown.
Add one half of stock to the roux and mix until smooth.
Add remaining stock, simmer 20–30 minutes.
Strain, season, and finish off with cream. Reserve.

Filling

Ingredients

1 1/2 lbs. (31/35 count)	Shrimp, cleaned, peeled, and deveined
24	Asparagus, trimmed, peeled, and cut into pieces
8 oz.	Mushrooms, sliced
3	Plum tomatoes, peeled, seeded, and diced
1/2 tbsp.	Olive oil
2 tsp.	Thyme, picked
1 tsp.	Parsley, chopped
1 tsp.	Chervil
To taste	Salt and pepper

Method

Blanch asparagus and sauté mushrooms in the oil.

Fold the herbs, defrosted shrimp, and all vegetables together with half of the sauce.

Grease six 6-oz. soufflé dishes, distribute filling evenly.

Top each dish with a 3-inch disk of your favorite pie dough.

Bake in a 350° oven until crust is brown, about 8–12 minutes.

Carnitas Monterey

*W*hen you're a chef and married, one of the first questions you likely will be asked at parties or gatherings is "Who does the cooking at home?" My wife also receives comments such as "Wow, you must be lucky to have him cook for you all the time!" People also assume that chefs are picky when dining out and act like restaurant critics every place they go: "Oh, it must be tough going out to eat with him!"

I cannot speak for every chef, but when I go out to eat I am going out to enjoy myself and not to measure a meal or a colleague. (The exception to this is if I am paying over $100 per person for dinner. Then you do expect it to be good!) Sometimes I go out to learn something and see what other chefs are creating or doing so I can borrow a concept or two. Otherwise, I just enjoy eating out and conversing with my family and friends.

I do love to cook at home and have my family enjoy the food I prepare for them with love and the hope of building a sense of values. There is nothing better than my little kids saying, "I want to help, Daddy. I want to help!" My wife, on the other hand, will make sure that there is something else important to do when I start cooking.

My wife was born in Monterey, Mexico, and lived there for more than 12 years. Mexico never receives enough credit for its contribution to cuisine and the quality of its great-tasting food (think of vanilla and chocolate, for example). Fine dining restaurants with a Mexican menu are a rare find, and it is a shame because Mexico truly offers magnificent-tasting, complex food. Mole sauce, for instance, has more than 16 ingredients that all complement each other to make a great tasting sauce. Any country that can marry that many ingredients together for wonderful food has my respect.

My wife does cook and is a much better at it than she thinks. She has a very good palate, enjoys fine dining, and has a cuisine heritage I find valuable. Cooking for the kids is fun for her. For me, the task seems to be less exciting. What people do not realize is that chefs enjoy simple, tasty home cooking and look forward to this more than anything else at times. We all need a break from fancy presentations, sauces, and on-the-edge creativity. A great meatloaf with fluffy mashed potatoes, pan gravy, and fresh caramelized broccoli can be a real treat.

Sometimes I do the shopping or bring home an item from work the few special times I can be home at dinner hour. One day I called and said I would be home to join my family for dinner and asked my wife if she would start dinner. I would finish it when I got home. I received a nervous "yes" and proceeded to give the instructions.

We were going to have a flavorful slow-roasted pork butt that I had precooked and placed in a vacuum bag. In Mexico they call this *carnitas*. Let me tell you, there is nothing tastier than a seasoned pork butt that has been slow roasted for 5 to 6 hours and finished with high heat to create a crispy crust with tender, juicy and flavorful meat inside. It may take longer to cook than a center cut pork loin, but with a little more TLC it is all worth it when you take that first bite and think you are in culinary heaven.

When I came home I went into the kitchen. The rice was on the stove, my adobe sauce was simmering, and the vegetables were ready to be cooked. It also would be served with some black beans that had been cooked for 10 hours with pork shanks, garlic, onions, and a flavorful broth. This was to be a great meal. I was getting excited; just the thought of those items teamed up with crispy and moist *carnitas* had me rocking.

Then I smelled something a bit off, and I checked to see what it was. I opened the oven door to check the pork and see if the smell was coming from there. As the door opened, my mouth dropped open as well. I yelled for my wife as I stood there in disbelief.

My *carnitas* was in the oven at 375° as I had asked. It was on a rack in a roasting pan as I had asked. However, it was still in the vacuum bag! My wife looked at me like I was nuts and asked what all the fuss was about. She said she thought I said to leave it in the bag. Then she blamed me for making her nervous in the kitchen and said that this was why she does not cook for me, nor should anyone else for that matter. I do admit I can be a bit fussy, but a plastic bag being cooked over my meat gave me reason to make some comments.

I was not sure whether the couch was going to be my bed for the night, but a great dinner of Carnitas Monterey (a new dish created by my wife minus the bag) and fine wine made everything okay.

Please enjoy the recipes that follow this story and savor the flavors of Mexican cuisine, as it has so much to offer. One should always try and seek out the real tastes and cooking methods of different countries so one can appreciate true flavors that will tantalize the tastebuds.

Fresh Banana Fritters
(About 1½ pints)

Ingredients

2	Eggs
1 oz.	Sugar
6 fluid oz.	White wine
6 fluid oz.	Apple juice
Pinch	Salt
1/2 tsp	Lemon rind, blanched, chopped
1/2 tsp.	Orange rind, blanched, chopped
12 oz.	All-purpose flour, sifted
2 lbs.	Bananas cut into pieces

Method

To make the batter, combine eggs and sugar, and whip lightly.
Add wine, apple juice, salt, and rinds.
Add flour; blend until smooth.
Dip fruit in batter; deep-fry at 350° until golden brown and drain on absorbent paper.
Serve with fruit sauce or whipped cream as desired.

Tamales
(16 tamales)

Tamale Dough

Ingredients

2 cups	Maseca
2 cups	Chicken broth or vegetable broth, lukewarm
1 tsp.	Baking powder
3/4 tsp.	Kosher salt
2/3 cup	Lard

Method

Combine maseca, baking powder, and salt in a bowl.
Work in broth to make a moist dough.
Beat lard until fluffy.
Add dough and beat until dough has a spongy texture.

Filling

Ingredients

2 lbs.	Pork shoulder
10 oz.	Mirepoix (diced celery, carrots, and onions)
1/2 oz.	Dried chilis
3 oz.	Olive oil blend or corn oil
6 oz.	Chicken or pork broth
1/2 tbsp.	Kosher salt
16	Corn husks
2 1/2 lbs.	Masa dough

Method

Roast pork shoulder in 400° oven for 10–15 minutes.
Place in pot with mirepoix and cover with a flavorful chicken broth.
Bring to a boil, simmer for 2–3 hours until meat falls off the bone tender.
Reserve.
Sauté cleaned chili pods in oil.
Combine chili pods and oil in a blender and blend until smooth.
Remove meat from bone in shreds.

Sauté meat until lightly browned.

Add chili mixture to meat; season with kosher salt.

To make tamales, place mixture in corn husks and roll to form a tight package. Place carefully in a steamer and cook for approximately 1 hour.

Crème Caramel
(14 servings)

Ingredients

8 oz.	Sugar
Few drops	Lemon juice, fresh
3 fluid oz.	Water
1 qt.	Milk
8 oz.	Sugar
1	Vanilla bean
4	Egg yolks
6	Eggs, beaten

Method

Butter the sides of 14 ramekins.

Combine the sugar, lemon juice, and water for the caramel and cook to a rich brown,

Carefully divide among the bottoms of ramekins.

Bring milk and 4 oz. of sugar to a boil; remove from heat. (If using a vanilla bean, steep it in the hot milk mixture.)

Combine the egg yolks and the remaining sugar; stir well.

Temper the eggs with hot milk. Do not return to the heat.

Divide the custard mixture among the ramekins.

Place the ramekins in a bain marie; place in a 325° oven.

Bake for approximately 35 minutes or until the custard has set.

Refrigerate overnight before turning out and serving.

Note: To temper the eggyolk mixture, add hot milk slowly while whisking constantly. This will prevent the eggyolks from curdling and cooking. The *baine marie* is a pan filled with water $1/3$ of the way up the ramekins. This keeps the crème caramel from cooking too fast and curdling.

Gazpacho
(12 servings)

Ingredients

2 cups	Rich vegetable stock
3 oz.	Olive oil
1 clove	Garlic, minced
4 oz.	Tomato paste
1 tsp.	Salt
1/2 tsp.	Pepper
1 lb.	Red pepper, roasted
1 lb.	Cucumber, peeled and seeded
1/2 lb.	Shallots, peeled
3 oz.	Balsamic vinegar
1	Juice of 2 limes
5 oz.	Virgin olive oil
2 cups	V-8 juice
1/2 tbsp.	Cilantro, minced
1 tbsp.	Parsley, chopped
1 tsp.	Cayenne pepper
To taste	Kosher salt
6	Plum tomatoes, peeled, seeded, and diced small
3/4 cup	Cucumbers, peeled, seeded, and diced small
1 cup	Yellow peppers, roasted and diced small
1/2 cup	Scallions, sliced thin
1 cup	Brioche croutons

Method

Heat stock in soup pot.
Heat olive oil in sauté pan, add garlic, cook 1–2 minutes then add paste and salt and pepper, cook well without browning.
Add to stock mix then simmer 15–20 minutes, cool in ice bath.
In a high-speed blender, process pepper, cucumbers, and shallots.
Mix all liquid ingredients; slowly pour into blender.
Add to stock.
Season soup.
Garnish with vegetables and brioche croutons.

Test of the Masters I

*I*n 1996, I decided it was time to take the test to become a master chef. This exam has a failure rate of 65% and covers all areas of cookery, including classical, American, baking, and so on. The exam is 10 days long and can wear on you both mentally and physically. It is a combination of mostly cookery and some theoretical subjects, such as financial management, supervisory skills, and so on.

To help myself prepare for the exam, I went back to the basics. I took a job at a restaurant with my friend Chef Brad Barnes, who would study with me and take the exam as well. We worked the hot line, butchered meat and fish, and did anything else that we needed to do to remember the basics and make them second nature to us for the exam.

On the third day of the exam, I was still there. So far, so good. The day for the supervisory and human resource management portion of the test came. This would be a breeze for me; I had many years of experience managing large crews and staffs, and I had worked as a director of food and beverage operations for a few years.

The class began, and the professor gave us an hour-long lecture on working with people and managing situations. He then handed out the test and told us to review and start in 5 minutes.

I could not wait to start the test and then take a break prior to the cooking segment in the afternoon. I went through all the questions, answering each with care, confident that I knew the answers. The exam presented questions and situations that you were to respond to in essay form in 50 words or fewer.

After half an hour or more, other chefs in class started getting up and handing in their papers. My friend Brad got up to hand in his test and gave me a puzzled look as if to say, "What is going on? You are supposed be the one who knows this stuff inside and out."

A few more minutes went by and I was the only one left in the class. I looked out the window. Everyone was relaxing or studying, and Brad looked at me puzzled again.

I finished, handed in my paper, and started to collect my things. The professor said, "Chef Leonard, wait a second. Did you not read the whole test?" I responded with a confused look and said, "I think so."

"Well," he said, "you answered every question on every page when at the top of each page it said to select two questions out of the five to answer."

I stood there with mixed emotions and realized why I was the last one to finish.

With a hopeful look I said, "Do I get extra credit for answering them all?" The professor moved his head slightly upward, looked down his glasses, and said "No. Perhaps I should grade you on the ability to understand and listen."

Boy, the test of the masters was not going to be an easy one; more focus was indeed needed on my part.

Edward Christopher's Pan-Roasted Sea Bass with Olive Oil Tomatoes
(6 servings)

Ingredients

6 portions	Black or Chilean sea bass, 6–8 oz. each, skin removed
To taste	Sea salt or kosher salt
To taste	Freshly ground black pepper
3 oz.	Virgin olive oil
4 sprigs	Thyme
2 tsp.	Spice de Cosette seasoning
	Juice of 2 limes
1 tbsp.	Honey
4 oz.	White wine
1	Lemon
2 oz.	Butter, diced

Method

Pat sea bass filets dry.

Mix sea salt, pepper, virgin olive oil, thyme, Spice de Cosette, lime juice, and honey well in a bowl.

Add sea bass filets and toss, coating all filets well.

Cover and let sit for 20–30 minutes.

Over high heat, heat a cast iron skillet or heavy-bottomed sauté pan that has been seasoned, or use a nonstick pan.

Place filets skin side up and cook for 3–4 minutes until nicely browned.

Turn over and cook 2–3 minutes more.

Deglaze pan with white wine, top fish with butter and a squeeze of juice from the lemon.

Place in 350° oven for 4–5 minutes, until fish is flaky and just cooked through.

Serve with Caramelized Onion and Potato Tart and Olive Oil Tomatoes.

Caramelized Onion and Potato Tart
(6 servings)

Ingredients

2 oz.	Butter
1 oz.	Oil
2 tsp.	Sugar
2 medium	Onions, finely sliced
1 clove	Garlic, crushed and peeled
2 oz.	Sweet white wine or white grape juice
6 pieces	Puff pastry, cut 4 × 2¹/₂ inches
3	Yukon gold potatoes, peeled and cooked
To taste	Salt and pepper
4 oz.	Butter, melted

Method

Place a sauté pan on medium to high heat and add the butter and oil.

When butter melts, add the sugar, then the garlic and the onions.

Cook, tossing every 2–3 minutes, until onions are nice and brown and the pan is caramelized.

Deglaze the pan with wine and cook until dry; cool down.

On a greased tray or one lined with nonstick baking paper, place squares of puff pastry.

Prick pastry with a fork.

Brush pastry with the melted butter, then divide onions and spread out on pastry.

Toss the slices of potatoes with remaining butter and season lightly with salt and pepper.

Arrange potato slices equally over pastry squares.

Place in a 350° oven and bake 10–12 minutes, or until pastry is golden brown.

Serve with lamb, fish, or roasted chicken breast.

Olive Oil Tomatoes for Fish Dishes

Ingredients

2 tbsp.	Salt
6 large	Roma tomatoes
10–12 oz.	Extra virgin olive oil
3	White anchovy fillets
4 sprigs	Thyme
1 tsp.	Fennel seeds, crushed

Method

Fill a 3–4 qt. saucepan with water half way and add 2 tbsp. salt. Heat to boiling.

On the top of each tomato, make a small X with a sharp paring knife.

Submerge tomatoes in boiling water and let boil for 30 seconds.

Remove tomatoes and place in a small bowl with ice water. Pat dry after cooling.

Remove the skin from each tomato and then cut into fours.

Remove the seeds and pulps, and you have 24 tomato petals.

Place the tomato petals on the bottom of a small pot; add the anchovy fillets, thyme, fennel seeds, and oil, making sure it is enough to cover.

Bring the oil to a low heat (150°–160°) and let the tomatoes sit constant at that heat for 2 hours.

If petals are still firm but tender, they are done; if not, cook for another 15–30 minutes.

Remove tomatoes, place in a dish, spoon 2–4 tbsp. of oil over them, and keep warm.

You can strain the oil and keep it in the refrigerator to use again or for a salad dressing.

Serve tomatoes over the top of fish dishes, on fish pasta dishes, or on crostini served with fish stews.

Chicken Giancarlo with Vinegar Peppers, Olive Oil Potatoes, and Candied Garlic
(4 servings)

Ingredients

2	Free Range chickens, cut in 8 pieces
1/2 cup	Kosher salt
To cover	Water
To taste	Salt and pepper
3 tbsp.	Naples spice rub (Chefnique brand)
3 tbsp.	Butter
1 tbsp.	Olive oil
As needed	Flour
As needed	Grapeseed oil

Method

The night before, soak chicken pieces in salted water.

Remove the chicken pieces, rinse, and pat dry well with paper towel.

In a bowl, combine salt and pepper, spice rub, butter, olive oil, and the chicken; toss until chicken is well coated with herbs and oil.

In a cast iron skillet or heavy bottomed pan, add grapeseed oil to about 1/3 of the depth of the pan and place on medium to high heat.

Dust chicken pieces in flour and place in pan; cook until nicely brown on all sides, about 3–4 minutes per side.

Remove from pan and put chicken pieces in a large bowl.

Add 16 vinegar peppers, one recipe of candied garlic, and olive oil potatoes (recipes follow).

Toss all items well and place in a roasting pan with a drizzle of very good extra virgin olive oil.

Place in a 375° oven and cook for about 8–10 minutes until the flavors marry and the chicken is just cooked.

Enjoy.

Candied Garlic
(2 pounds)

Ingredients

1 qt.	Water
1 qt.	Sugar
2 lbs.	Garlic cloves, peeled and cleaned

Method

Bring water and sugar to a boil and simmer 15 minutes.
Add garlic, simmer until tender but not soft.
Drain.
Place garlic on Silpat or baking paper and bake in 375° oven until very light color is achieved.

Uncle Dominic's Vinegar Peppers

Ingredients

16	Red and green cherry peppers
1 oz.	Olive oil
2 cups	Aged red wine vinegar
4 oz.	Balsamic vinegar
2 tbsp.	Red pepper flakes
1 tbsp.	Sugar

Method

Sauté peppers in oil in a heated sauté pan for 2–3 minutes.

Add 1 cup of the red wine vinegar.

In a stainless steel saucepan, add remaining red wine vinegar and balsamic vinegar to red pepper flakes and sugar. Bring to a low boil.

Place peppers in the vinegar and let simmer for 2–3 minutes.

Let steep and cool down for 6–10 minutes.

Place in a jar, cover, and refrigerate.

Use peppers as they are with pork and chicken dishes, or sauté them.

Olive Oil Potatoes
(6 servings)

Ingredients

2 lbs.	Yukon Gold potatoes
As needed	Salt
4–6 qts.	Water
4 oz.	Good olive oil
2 oz.	Butter, melted
To taste	Salt and pepper
2 tsp.	Dried oregano

Method

Place potatoes in a soup pot with well-salted water that covers the potatoes by more than 2 inches.

Bring the water to a boil, and cook the potatoes until just tender but still a bit firm.

Drain well, and place on a tray to cool.

Remove skins.

Cube potatoes into $1/2$-inch cubes.

In a bowl, toss potatoes with oil, butter, salt and pepper, and oregano.

Place on a tray rubbed with some olive oil, and drizzle oil from the bowl over the potatoes.

Bake in a 375° oven, turning every 4–5 minutes, until golden brown.

Serve with roasted meats or fish.

Test of the Masters II

Where Are the Beans?

*I*t was Day 10, the final day of the master chef's exam. I had made it with a comfortable passing grade so far, after nine days of receiving my lumps and bruises. If I could pass the next two cooking segments, I would wear the CMC pin and become one of only 55 Certified Master Chefs in the United States!

The exam was tough and tested every aspect of practical skills in the culinary arts. This last day was worth 50% of the grade. All this work after nine days, and 50% of the final grade depended on my passing these next two segments with a 75% grade or better! For the first segment I had to produce 10 portions of a three-course international menu (Spanish) in $3^1/2$ hours from start to finish. Then, after a quick bite to eat and a short rest period, the dreaded mystery basket test would take place. This is the test many chefs have failed throughout the history of the exam. For the mystery basket exam, a basket of food is given to you and you have 30 minutes to write a menu for a three-course meal that will be served to CMC tasting judges sequestered in a private room.

I went into the kitchen ready to prepare my three courses of black bean soup, rolled and stuffed flank steak (Datum), and a refreshing salad of vegetables with plantains for the first segment of this part of the exam. Each of us had $4^1/2$ hours to cook the 30 portions from the start of butchery to the final service. Once your window (service time) was called, you had 20 minutes to plate all 30 portions in the best possible manner. Your meal would be judged on taste and your skill level.

I worked fast and efficiently, concentrating every step of the way on flavor, following proper cooking techniques, and so on. I was especially proud of the soup. It was a simple soup to prepare, but how was I going to make a simple soup impress and excite the tastebuds of five Certified Master Chefs locked away in the judging room?

My plan was to focus on the presentation and service. Each bowl would be garnished with very tiny diced vegetables—onions, peppers, and such. Of course, I also would reserve a bowl of cooked black beans to purée and add to the soup as a final touch. Then, quenelles of sour cream, pluches (buds picked off the stem) of cilantro, and a drizzle of very high grade extra virgin olive oil would bring the dish to life!

For service, the empty bowls would be garnished and the soup poured at the table in front of the judges. Oh man, the aroma! This presentation would make you want to jump into the bowl! I could picture the chefs eating and talking about my soup saying, "Now this is a soup from a master."

All went well. The garnish was ready, plates were hot, my flank steak was perfect and resting on the stove, and the salad was marinating and raring to go. I had the final ingredients ready. I was moving among the stoves, tasting and adjusting for any last-minute improvements while the tasting judge stood by and watched.

The kitchen judge then said, "Chef, your window is open."

Those 20 minutes went by so fast I did not know what happened. Every dish was leaving, the station was being kept clean, food was being served with love and passion. "This is what it is about," I said. I loved the rush.

I made it with a minute to spare. The students serving came back and said, "Nice job, Chef. They are all eating and enjoying the food."

The kitchen judge came by and said, "Nice job Chef, that's the way to go."

My apprentice and I started cleaning so my station would be ready for the mystery basket in 1 hour. As we cleaned the fridge, I noticed the bowl of pureed black beans still in the cooler. I had forgotten and left them out of the soup.

I was now nervous. Was this mistake going to affect my grade? Were they expecting whole black beans? What about the kitchen judge? He saw me marinate them and watched me plate up. What was I to do?

The kitchen judge was coming to do a final check. I kept the door open to the cooler to block anyone from seeing me, and I ate that bowl of black beans so fast that I think I swallowed the whole bowl like a shot glass of whiskey from a bar.

It did not sit well with me. The judge flew around my corner, checked my box, checked my coolers, and then asked, "Where are those beans, Chef?"

"What beans?" I replied, as my stomach was still digesting and my breath felt like a talking marinade of garlic and onions.

"I do not believe that I saw you put them in the bowl when serving your soup."

"You must have," I said. "They are gone." He checked the garbage and seemed to be satisfied with the fact that they were gone, at least for now.

That night my stomach was to make me regret devouring this bowl of beans. It stayed with me for some time to come, if you know what I mean.

However, the test of the masters did as well. I received a very high scor—in the 90s—for my Spanish menu and did well enough with the basket to receive the coveted Certified Master Chef pin.

I put myself through a test to see what I was made of—to see if my apprenticeship, the dreams I had along the way, and the fortunate positions I had in the industry were well deserved or not. It was a proud moment at a very tough time in my life. It is a moment that I will always do my best to live up to by giving back to the craft and helping others reach their goals and dreams.

In life, success is only as good as what is given back to others so they to may have a chance to be what they want to be as well. Cooking is a true love of mine, a passion that has burned for years and keeps burning. I hope that as you have read these tales, and perhaps tried some of these nice recipes, you will have another love in your life as well.

Shrimp and Wild Mushroom Crostini
(6 servings)

Shrimp

Ingredients

36 (16/20 count)	Shrimp, peeled and deveined
4 oz.	Extra virgin olive oil
2 tbsp.	Picked thyme
2 tbsp.	Honey
½ tsp.	Pepper, freshly ground
2	Lemons, cut in half
2	Limes, cut in half
2 oz.	Butter, diced
2 tbsp.	Extra virgin olive oil
1 tbsp.	Parsley, chopped

Method

Thoroughly mix olive oil, thyme, honey, and pepper in a bowl.
Squeeze juice from lemons and limes into bowl.
Add shrimp plus the lemon and lime halves.
Toss shrimp and coat well with marinade. Let sit at room temperature for 20–30 minutes.
Grill shrimp on each side until just finished. Do not overcook.
In a bowl, toss shrimp, butter, and olive oil with the chopped parsley while still warm.

Mushrooms

Ingredients

18 oz.	Assortment of wild mushrooms, cleaned and cut
2	Shallots, minced
3 tbsp.	Olive oil
2 oz.	Sweet butter
2 tbsp.	Fresh tarragon, minced
1 oz.	Butter, diced

Method

In a sauté pan, add olive oil and butter, sweat shallots until soft, then add mushrooms.
Cook for 3–4 minutes until mushrooms are soft.
Add tarragon and butter.
Remove from heat and toss.

Crostini

Ingredients

18 pieces	High-quality semolina bread, cut on bias, ½ inch thick
4 cloves	Garlic, peeled and cut in half
As needed	Extra virgin olive oil

Method

Rub bread slices with garlic, then brush each side with extra virgin olive oil.
Grill bread on slow grill, then finish in 350°–375° oven until lightly toasted.

Balsamic Syrup

Ingredients

1 cup	Balsamic vinegar
2 oz.	Honey
1 tbsp.	Sugar

Method

Combine all ingredients in a stainless steel pan.
Reduce by half over medium heat.
Cool in refrigerator.

Assembly

Arrange six plates with three slices of bread each.
Spoon equal amounts of mushrooms on each and drizzle any remaining juice over them.
Place two shrimp on each slice of bread and drizzle any remaining butter and oil over shrimp.
Lace plate with balsamic syrup.

Puerto Rican Style Arroz con Pollo
(4 servings)

Ingredients

2¹/₂ lbs.	Chicken quarters
5 cloves	Garlic, minced
1 tbsp.	Oregano
¹/₂ tbsp.	Kosher salt
1 tsp.	Black pepper
3 oz.	Olive oil
1 oz.	Red wine vinegar
3 oz.	Butter
8 oz.	Onions, diced
8 oz.	Carrots diced
4 oz.	Smoked ham
5 oz.	Red wine
2 tbsp.	Chili peppers, minced
6 oz.	Green olives with pimientos, diced
2 cups	Uncooked rice
4 cups	Chicken broth
¹/₂ cup	Plum tomatoes, diced
¹/₂ oz.	Cilantro leaves, chopped
1 cup	Frozen peas
12 spears	Asparagus, cooked and chopped
2 oz.	Olive oil
To taste	Salt and pepper

Method

Toss chicken pieces with garlic, oregano, ¹/₂ tbsp. kosher salt, 1 tsp. black pepper, 3 oz. olive oil, and red wine vinegar. Let sit for 1 hour.
Place in a pan and roast in a 425° oven for 8–10 minutes.
Remove from pan.
Scrape pan and fat into a bowl and reserve.
Melt butter in a 4-qt brazier pot.
Add onions, carrots, and ham; sauté until light brown.
Deglaze with red wine.
Add chili peppers, olives, and rice, and cook 2–3 minutes, stirring.
Add broth, chicken pieces, and reserved fat.

Cover pot and cook in a 350° oven for 15–20 minutes until rice has absorbed liquid and cooked.

Remove chicken.

Fold in all other ingredients.

Serve rice and vegetables with 2 pieces of chicken per serving.

Master's Pie Crust
(two 9-inch crusts)

Ingredients

3 cups	All-purpose flour
1 tsp.	Salt
2 tbsp.	Sugar
16 tbsp.	Unsalted butter
8 tbsp.	All-vegetable shortening, cold
8 tbsp.	Ice water

Method

Mix flour, salt, and sugar in food processor with steel blade.

Dice butter into $1/4$-inch pieces.

Scatter over flour mixture and toss to cover butter with flour.

Cut into flour with 1-second pulses, 5 times.

Add shortening and repeat pulses about 4 times; should look like coarse cornmeal, and butter bits are pea size.

Turn into a bowl.

Sprinkle 6 tbsp. of ice water over mixture.

With a rubber spatula and a folding motion, combine and press on dough until dough sticks together. Add the other 1 or 2 tbsp. of water if needed.

Shape into ball with hands, flatten into two 4-inch disks, dust with flour, and refrigerate for 1 hour prior to rolling.

Dried Fruit and Chocolate BBQ Sauce
(4 cups)

Ingredients

1/2 cup	Golden raisins
1/4 cup	Dried apple, diced small
1/4 cup	Dried pear, diced small
1/4 cup	Dried banana slices
1/4 cup	Dried apricot, chopped
2 sticks	Cinnamon
2 tbsp.	Brown sugar
3/4 cup	Rum
4 tbsp.	Olive oil
4 cloves	Garlic, minced
1/2 cup	Onions, minced
4	Apples, diced
4 slices	Bacon, cooked and diced
3 tbsp.	High-quality cocoa
1 cup	Ketchup
2 tbsp.	Mustard
4 tbsp.	Brown sugar
3 oz.	Cider Vinegar

Method

Marinate first 7 ingredients in rum and let sit for 60 minutes. Remove cinnamon sticks.

Heat oil in a sauté pan and cook garlic, onions, apples, and bacon for 3–4 minutes.

Add to remaining ingredients in a blender or food processor; pulse for 2–3 minutes.

Place in a saucepan.

Add to fruit mixture and rum.

Place on stove and bring to a boil, mixing well.

Let simmer 15–20 minutes on low heat.

Let cool.

Use for baby back ribs, chicken, and pulled pork.

Almond Chocolate Cake
(one 9-inch cake)

Ingredients

10 oz.	Blanched almonds
2 tbsp.	Granulated sugar
4 oz.	Butter, at room temperature
10 oz.	Granulated sugar
6	Extra large eggs, separated and at room temperature
6 oz.	High-quality semisweet chocolate, grated
2 oz.	High-quality unsweetened cocoa powder
2 tbsp.	Palermo coffee, ground, or another high-quality coffee
2 oz.	Kahlúa
2 tbsp.	Real vanilla

Method

Toast almonds lightly on a sheet pan in a 350° oven. Watch carefully—
they burn quickly.

Cool, then place in food processor.

Add 2 tbsp. of sugar and pulse only until finely chopped.

Place butter and sugar in bowl and whip until creamy and fluffy.

Add egg yolks one at a time, beating well for each addition.

Add chocolate, cocoa, coffee, Kahlúa, and vanilla.

Beat until mixed, no more than 1 minute.

Fold in almonds.

Whip egg whites until creamy and stiff. Fold into batter in two stages.

Bake in a 9-inch springform pan that has been buttered and papered on
the bottom.

Bake in a 350° oven for 35–45 minutes until knife comes out clean.

Place on cake rack and cool 30 minutes.

Reader's Notes and Thoughts

Live to Eat

Americans have come far in their appreciation of food, but we still have a way to go to truly appreciate what food has to offer. We still need to understand what is right and wrong to eat and to educate ourselves that good, fresh food; good, fresh, real butter; and other products do have a place in our lives and on our tables. The fast and convenient way to eat is hurting us. Processed foods, oversized portions, and bad home-cooked meals point to a society crying out for culinary values to come back.

The dinner or supper table was always a place to bring family members together to talk and most of all enjoy home-cooked food. Many of the recipes that chefs create, cook, and put on a menu originated with home cooks at some point. Long before there were restaurants, people cooked in their homes using ingredients from local farmers and growers. Cooking was a family event, with people pitching in to help and perform different tasks.

Perhaps this practice of sitting down and enjoying dinner together as a family needs to come back. Perhaps taking the time to cook and showing people you care needs to be done through food. When people start suing chain restaurants for making them overweight, we know something has gone wrong. Perhaps if time is taken to ensure that our kids eat right and enjoy fresh-cooked food with fresh ingredients, things will be different.

During one of my visits to Italy, I went to a restaurant operated by five older Italian ladies. Every Sunday, reservations were taken only for groups of eight or more. Up to 200 guests would come and dine family style. These ladies cooked with only seasonal products that were available locally—end of story. There was no menu and there were no choices for customers to make. You came and you ate what was offered. And what was offered was 4 hours of the greatest seven-course dinner with wine that I have ever enjoyed.

Waiters would come out course after course and serve delicious, freshly made food. You could partake of a particular course or not; it was up to you. But missing a course would be a sin. People talked, laughed, drank, and spent quality time over a simple thing called food. We even took a short walk between two courses to take in the great view overlooking the city.

When the meal was over, I went to meet these chefs. To my surprise, there were five ladies in aprons, cooking, cleaning, and orchestrating the kitchen like magic. The aroma alone made me hungry all over again. We chatted, and one lady said, "Chef I feel a' bad for you."

"Why?" I inquired.

"Because you should a' be cooking here, not over there" (in the United States). She continued to say that she could feel my passion and excitement when we all talked about food, and she said, "You see, here in Italy we live to eat. In the United States they eat just to live, and that is so sad."

That conversation stuck with me. It caused me to think about the way I approach what I do and to try to give people a dining experience that will help them to look at food as an important part of their lives.

The chef was correct in a good part of what she said. Our quick dinners, quicker lunches, and habit of eating on the run don't allow us the time to enjoy food or life. Perhaps we should step back and start to live to eat, to enjoy, and to relish.

I hope *Tastes and Tales of a Chef* will at least cause you to think about this philosophy and the importance of food in our lives. Good cooking, and take the time to dine, not just to eat.

Grandma's Sunday Sauce
(8 servings)

Ingredients

1/4 cup	Olive oil
8 oz.	Stewing beef, diced
8 oz.	Italian sausage, cut in 1-inch slices
3	Garlic, peeled and sliced thin
8 oz.	Pork butt or shoulder, diced
1 small	Yellow onion, diced small
3 tbsp.	High-quality tomato paste
6 oz.	Dry red wine
4 cups	Canned Italian plum tomatoes, put through a food mill or blender
1/4 cup	Parmesan Reggiano cheese, grated
3	Fresh basil leaves
1 tsp.	Red pepper flakes
2 tbsp.	Parsley, chopped
3 tbsp.	Extra virgin olive oil

Method

Heat 1/4 cup olive oil in sauce pot (stainless steel is best).
Pat all meat dry, add to pot, and brown nicely.
Remove meat and place on a dish.
Add sliced garlic and onion; sauté until soft.
Add tomato paste and cook another 2–3 minutes.
Deglaze pan with red wine, mix well, and cook 1–2 minutes.
Add meat and juices and tomatoes, stir, and bring to a slow simmer.
After 1 hour, add remaining ingredients.
Simmer for another 60–90 minutes until meat is tender.
Season with salt and pepper to taste
Serve over your favorite pasta.

Cavatelli
(1 pound of pasta, 4 servings)

Ingredients

4 cups	Flour
1 tsp.	Salt
1¹/₄ cups	Water, lukewarm

Method

Place flour and salt in a large bowl.

Add lukewarm water and stir with spoon until mixed.

Turn out onto floured board and work dough with hands for 20–30 minutes until thoroughly mixed.

Cover dough with a bowl and let it rest for 1–2 hours. Flour board and roll small piece of dough until it is about ¼ inch thick.

Cut into ³/₄-inch strips and cut strips into 1¹/₂ inch pieces.

Take a little piece and place your second and third fingers on it; then bear down and roll dough at the same time.

Keep repeating this until all the dough is used up.

Flour and spread over the board until ready to cook.

Cook in boiling, salted water 25 minutes. Serve.

Manicotti
(8–10 servings)

Batter

Ingredients

8	Eggs
2 cups	Flour
2 cups	Water
Pinch	Salt
As needed	Melted butter or olive oil

Method

Beat eggs with mixer at low speed. Add flour gradually into mixing bowl, then add water slowly.

In a nonstick pan over medium heat, make 6-inch pasta crepes with batter, brushing pan with oil or butter in between.

Filling

Ingredients

2 lbs.	Ricotta cheese
To taste	Kosher salt
1/2 cup	Reggiano-Parmesan cheese
1/2 cup	Parsley, chopped
2 1/2 cups	Fresh mozzarella, diced small
2	Eggs

Method

Combine all ingredients and mix well.

Assembly

Place pasta crepes on a table. Divide the filling equally among the crepes and roll well.

Ladle your favorite tomato sauce into an oven-proof dish, then place manicotti in the dish.

Bake in 350° oven for 8–12 minutes.

Duck Ragù
(4 cups)

Ingredients

4 lbs.	Duck legs and thighs
1/4 cup	Olive oil
2 oz.	Butter
1 oz.	Duck fat
1/2 oz.	Dried porcini mushrooms, soaked in warm water for 30 minutes
1 small	Onion, diced small
3	Carrots, diced small
2 cloves	Garlic, sliced thin
1/2 cup	Oyster mushrooms, trimmed and cut
1/2 cup	Fresh or canned tomatoes, diced
2 oz.	Tomato paste
1/2 cup	Red wine
1 cup	Veal demi-glace or veal broth
1/2 cup	Golden raisins, soaked in warm water
To taste	Salt and pepper

Method

In a large pan, sauté the duck pieces in the oil and butter as needed.
Remove and reserve when brown on both sides.
Add duck fat to pan.
Add drained and diced porcini (save liquid).
Add all other vegetables and sauté until soft.
Add tomato paste, cook out well, deglaze with wine.
Add duck legs, tomato, and raisins.
Cover pan and cook at 300° until tender.
Remove legs and thighs and pull meat.
Add back to sauce and season with salt and pepper.
Serve over a wide noodle pasta.

Vodka Cream Sauce
(8 servings)

Ingredients

1	Shallot, minced
1 clove	Garlic, minced
2 tbsp.	Butter
2 tbsp.	Olive oil
1/2 cup	Roma tomato, peeled, seeded, and diced
1/4 cup	Vodka
1/2 cup	Chicken broth
2 cups	Sauce pomodoro
1/2 cup	Mascarpone cheese
To taste	Salt and pepper

Method

Sauté shallot and garlic in oil and butter until soft.
Add tomato and cook for 2–3 minutes.
Pull pan from stove and add vodka.
Put pan back on stove and flame; cook 1–2 minutes.
Add broth and sauce pomodoro; simmer for 12–15 minutes.
Season with salt and pepper.
Quickly whip in the mascarpone cheese and toss with 1 lb. of penne pasta cooked al dente.

Amatriciana Sauce
(8 servings)

Ingredients

1 oz.	Olive oil
1/2 cup	Onion, minced
2 oz.	Pancetta, diced
2 tsp.	Red pepper flakes
4 oz.	Tomatoes, diced
2 cups	Tomato sauce

Method

In a saucepan, cook onion in oil until just brown.
Add pancetta and render well.
Add red pepper flakes; cook 2–3 minutes.
Add tomato; cook 3–4 minutes.
Add your favorite tomato sauce and simmer.
Serve over 1 lb. of spaghetti or bucatini pasta.

Tuscan Green Sauce
(2 cups)

Ingredients

2/3 cup	Walnuts
1 1/2 cups	Italian parsley leaves
1/4 cup	Fresh basil leaves
2 cloves	Garlic
2	Hard-boiled egg yolks
2/3 cup	Olive oil
3 tbsp.	Heavy cream
To taste	Salt and pepper

Method

Place first 4 items in a food processor and purée.

Add egg yolks; purée again.

Using the pulse switch, add oil in a slow stream until emulsified.

Add cream.

Season with salt and pepper and place in a squeeze bottle.

Toss with hot pasta or use for cold salads, grilled vegetables, carpaccio, or grilled chicken and other meats.

White Peach Balsamic Dressing
(1 quart)

Ingredients

1 cup	White peach purée or white peach nectar
1 cup	White balsamic vinegar
2 cups	Grapeseed oil
1 tbsp.	Mint, chopped
1 tbsp.	Basil, chopped
Pinch	Salt and pepper

Method

Mix all ingredients thoroughly.
Use over your favorite salad greens or grilled vegetables.

Reader's Notes and Thoughts

Summary and Thoughts from the Chef

These tales and recipes are just some of those I would like to share with you, the reader and lover of culinary arts. The journey from an apprentice to a master chef involves so much more than what is in this book.

I chose to cook for a living, a choice I have never regretted or looked back upon. For me, every day is a new adventure on a journey I am still taking and still learning from. I have been blessed to meet so many wonderful people—as well as some who are not so wonderful who have taught me how never to be. I have learned that when chefs get together the language barrier is broken by the simple thing we call food and our craft of preparing it. The friendships I have forged, the food I have made, and the places I have seen during my journey hold a special place in my life.

I still love to cook and spend my days doing so as Executive Chef of the Westchester Country Club in Rye, New York. In my job I have the opportunity to train so many others in all aspects of the kitchen. We are becoming an apprenticeship site so others will have the chance to start this journey and some day become masters of cookery.

For readers who are not in the profession, I hope you will laugh and understand just a bit better the road it takes for those who prepare your meals when you dine out. I hope you are inspired to try some of the recipes or use them as a starting point for creating your own recipes to please those you cook for. I hope you get up every morning with a desire to make a difference in people's lives with the good food you cook or by sharing this book so they may take the journey as well.

As I always say, good cooking, good living, and have a good life.

Chef Edward G. Leonard, CMC

Take the Time

Take the time to cook and bake from the heart with care
It is the source of why you are here.

Take the time to reflect every day
And have a passion for our craft in a big way.

Take the time to always learn and grow
You must always expand on what you already know.

Take the time to truly believe in yourself and what you can do
If you don't at first, then who will?

Take the time to respect the foods of our land
Besides cooking properly it is the true secret to a great dish at hand.

Take the time to treat all you meet with respect along the way
You never know when you may have to call on them some day.

Take the time to teach and share what you know
The reward back is two-fold.

Take the time to make a difference in all that you do
It is a rare privilege experienced by a few.

Take the chance to do what they say can't be done
Achieving such odds is the real fun.

Take the time to always be the best you can be
That is the only measure anyone should see.

Take time to laugh and have fun
A day is complete when this is done.

Take the time to balance your life, and as you reach for the stars,
Do not forget those who have helped from afar.

For all the accolades that will come your way
Will mean nothing at all if there is no one there for you at the end of the day.

Take the time and always be true,
For the only meaning of success is what pleases you.

Chef Edward G. Leonard, CMC, AAC 1994

Glossary

Bain marie An insert pan that goes into a pan with simmering water; prevents items such as custards and cream sauces from cooking too fast or burning.

Blind bake To bake a pie or pastry dough fully; usually done with parchment paper and beans or pie weights to ensure that the crust does not form bubbles.

Bolognese A traditional meat sauce from the Emilia Romagna region of Italy; traditionally includes chicken livers and milk as ingredients.

Braciola Rolled beef or pork seasoned, tied, and braised in tomato sauce.

Break [sauce] When a sauce curdles or separates.

Bucatini A type of pasta, long and spaghetti-like, but hollow.

ChefNique A quality spice and specialty company for cooks and chefs. E-mail chefniquecmc@aol.com for ordering information.

Chiboust A pastry cream with gelatin and whipped egg whites folded into it.

Chiffonade A type of cut; rolling herb or vegetable leaves together and slicing them into thin strips.

Clarified butter Butter that has been simmered on low heat; when it sits, the milk separates and settles at the bottom, leaving a clear butter that can be used for cooking without burning.

Choucroute Traditional German sauerkraut made from cabbage.

Demi-glace Veal stock that has been reduced slowly, usually two thirds of the way, leaving a rich stock with oil-like consistency.

Dock A pastry term meaning to put holes in dough before blind baking; lets air escape so the dough will not puff up.

Egg wash Eggs are mixed with milk (usually) and then brushed on dough prior to baking for a nice, shiny crust and finish.

Escoffier Considered the father of classical cuisine and one of the greatest chefs of his time, with a great vision of cuisine for the future.

Flame Add alcohol to a hot pan and then ignite it.

Frangipane A rich pastry cake made with almond paste.

Garde The cold kitchen or pantry.

Hot line The line in a kitchen where the hot dishes are prepared and served.

Ice bath Ice and water used to cool a product down after heating; many kitchens put their stock in a water bath to reduce it to a safe temperature.

Insalata Italian word for salad.

Mirepoix Traditionally, a mixture of 50% onion, 25% carrot, and 25% celery used to flavor stocks, sauces, and consommé; more modern versions use different vegetables and diced them very small for use in a served sauce.

Mother sauce There are five mother sauces in classical cooking, these sauces are the foundation from which most other sauces are made.

Naples Spice Rub A spice mix with flavors of Italy by ChefNique LLC.

Picked Herb buds have been taken from their stems.

Pluches The sprigs of herb plants such as thyme, oregano, etc.

Ragù A stew; items braised in a sauce that is thick like a stew featuring those items.

Rémoulade A traditional cold sauce used for cold shellfish dishes.

Roux Equal amounts of flour and fat used to thicken and flavor sauces.

Salamander A grill or broiler that heats from the top; used to brown items.

Sauce pomodoro Tomato sauce as it is called in Italy. *Marinara sauce* is a misused American term that does not apply to tomato sauce. *Marinara* means married to the sea; *sauce marinara* is a seafood sauce.

Simple syrup One part sugar and one part water, boiled on the stove to dissolve the sugar; it is used to marinate fruits, brush on cakes, and sweeten ice tea or dressings and is easier to use than undissolved sugar. Can also be flavored with cloves, vanilla, etc.

Spice de Cosette A spice for seafood and poultry dishes, salads, and sauces. Some chefs believe it is better than Old Bay seasoning. Can be purchased from ChefNique LLC.

Temper To slowly bring to desired temperature by slowly adding a cool product to a hot one so they come together.

Tulie A cookie batter that is spread thin, sometimes with a template, and baked; can be shaped into cups or curved when hot, and then dries to a fragile, crisp cookie.

Window [in competition] In a competition you have only so much time to do your cooking. When the window opens, that means it is time to start serving your food.

Index